GETTING STARTED IN

OPTIONS

ILLUSTRATED EDITION

GETTING STARTED IN

OPTIONS

ILLUSTRATED EDITION

MICHAEL C. THOMSETT

WILEY

Other Wiley Editorial Offices
John Wiley & Sons, 111 River Street, Hoboken, NJ 07030, USA
John Wiley & Sons, The Atrium, Southern Gate, Chichester, West Sussex, P019 8SQ, United Kingdom
John Wiley& Sons (Canada) Ltd., 5353 Dundas Street West, Suite 400, Toronto, Ontario, M9B 6HB, Canada
John Wiley& Sons Australia Ltd., 42 McDougall Street, Milton, Queensland 4064, Australia
Wiley-VCH, Boschstrasse 12, D-69469 Weinheim, Germany

ISBN 978-1-118-39930-9 (Paperback)
ISBN 978-1-118-39926-2 (ePDF)
ISBN 978-1-118-39932-3 (Mobi)
ISBN 978-1-118-39931-6 (ePub)

Typeset in 11pt. Adobe Garamond Pro.
Printed in the United States

10 9 8 7 6 5 4 3 2

CONTENTS

ACKNOWLEGMENTS

Thanks to those many readers who wrote to offer their suggestions for and insights into previous editions of this book, including constructive criticism and clarifying questions. Their letters have helped to improve the ever-changing sets of explanations and examples, definitions, and other materials used in this book.

Very special thanks go to Debra Englander, my editor for many years at John Wiley & Sons, whose encouragement through many editions of this and other books has been greatly appreciated.

Also, many thanks to Nick Wallwork and Gemma Rosey, my editors in Singapore, for their excellent help and guidance through the production process.

ELEMENT KEY

Definitions
This symbol is found in boxed notations providing specific definitions of options terms. These are placed within the book to accompany and augment discussions relevant to each definition

Key Points
These highlighted sections emphasize key points or add observations, rules of thumb, resources, and added points that options traders can use.

Valuable Resources
These sections provide links to websites where you will find added value for particular options discussions, to further help in expanding your options knowledge base.

Examples
Numerous examples illustrate points raised in context and provide a view of how the issues might apply using actual options trades. This is intended to demonstrate practical application of the principles being presented.

INTRODUCTION

This edition is a departure from past evolution. In the past, editions were simply updated as new information evolved in the ever-changing options market. This new, illustrated edition contains many new elements and features not found in previous ones.

When the first edition of this book was published in 1989, the options market was very young and new. During that year, only 227 million contracts traded. Today, annual trading exceeds 4 billion contracts.

In the early days of this market, there was no Internet or affordable online order execution. The Internet has drastically changed all markets, including options, and has made them accessible to anyone with a PC or hand-held device. To give you an idea of how much matters have improved, today the clearing fees charged by the Options Clearing Corporation (OCC) are less than half of what they were before the year 2000.

The popularity of options trading is due to many factors. The market has grown up over the past two-plus decades. The investing and trading public consists of a broad range of people. Speculators are only a part of the overall options market today, expanding the importance of the options market into many areas beyond high-risk. Options may be either high-risk or extremely conservative, and can be used for portfolio management. This means that risks can be reduced and even eliminated with a carefully structured series of strategies aimed at offsetting downside risk.

The combination of Internet access and lower costs has combined to bring options to anyone and everyone who wants to find out how to use calls and puts as strategic tools. Product types have expanded throughout the period as well and today options are available not only on listed stocks, but also on indexes, exchange-traded funds (ETFs), and futures. Education has expanded as well. As options have become appealing to a wider range of investors and traders, industry experts and organizations like the OCC and the Chicago Board Options Exchange (CBOE) have vastly expanded their educational outreach.

This illustrated edition is designed with many new features. The book includes numerous examples, definitions in context, key points, website links, checklists, illustrations, and tables.

Anyone using this book to learn about options may appreciate that it includes some repetition. This is a device intended to help you to overcome the inherent complexity of options trading. The jargon is confusing at first, so it takes time to become accustomed to the new language of options. Making it even more difficult to quickly move into the market, the range of possible strategies is vast and this makes it important to take time to learn about options in steps.

Some suggestions for anyone new to this field:

- Master the terminology. Focus on the many specialized option terms and get accustomed to seeing them in the context of examples and strategies.
- Remember the context of risk. All investing and trading decisions are wisely made with an appreciation of the risk levels involved. Only by remembering risk can you know whether a strategy is appropriate for you.
- Track both options and stocks on the market. Options traders need to observe how options change in value in relation to how stocks move in price, especially when markets are volatile. You will discover that options do not track stock price changes exactly; there are many factors influencing how options pricing changes.
- Know yourself and what risks you can afford. It is all too easy for new options traders to be attracted to some strategies, even those that are too risky for them. So it is crucial that you know what you can afford, and what level of risk exposure works for you. This suggestion will make it more likely for you to succeed. Options work in the context of your own risk profile, and that is the key to any successful program.

The John Wiley & Sons Getting Started series is designed to help investors and traders overcome the complexity of markets. This is achieved with great teaching aids. These include carefully placed definitions, dozens of examples, illustrations, and more. The success of this series is due to the careful and thorough design of the many books in the series, and its emphasis on ease of use and provision of a lot of information. The Getting Started books are designed with you, the reader, in mind.

GETTING STARTED IN

OPTIONS

ILLUSTRATED EDITION

1 CALLS & PUTS: DEFINING THE FIELDS OF PLAY

> *Nine-tenths of wisdom is being wise in time.*
> —Theodore Roosevelt, speech, June 14, 1917

Options are amazing tools that can help you expand your control over your portfolio, protect positions, reduce market risk, and enhance current income. Some strategies are very high risk, but others are extremely conservative. This is what makes the options market so interesting. The variety of creative uses of options makes it possible to tie in profits in the most uncertain of conditions, or to pursue income opportunities without being exposed to even the most volatile markets.

Because the option is an intangible device, its cost is only a fraction of stock prices. This makes it possible to control shares of stock without assuming the market risks. Each option controls 100 shares, so for approximately 10 percent of the cost of buying shares in a company, you can use options to create the same profit stream. This makes your capital go farther while keeping risks very low.

This idea—using intangible contracts to duplicate the returns you expect from well-picked stocks—is revolutionary to anyone who has

equity investment

An investment in the form of part ownership, such as the purchase of shares of stock in a corporation.

never explored options trading. Most people are aware of the two best-known ways to invest money: equity and debt. An *equity investment* is the purchase of *a share* of stock or many shares of stock, which represents a partial interest in the company itself. Shares are sold through stock exchanges or over the counter (trades made on companies not listed on an exchange). For example, if a company has one million shares outstanding and you buy 100 shares, you own 100/1,000,000ths, or .0001 percent of the company.

When you buy 100 shares of stock, you are in complete control over that investment. You decide how long to hold the shares and when to sell. Stocks provide you with tangible value, because they represent part ownership in the company. Owning stock entitles you to dividends if they are declared, and gives you the right to vote in elections offered to stockholders. (Some special nonvoting stock lacks this right.) If the stock rises in value, you will gain a profit. If you wish, you can keep the stock for many years, even for your whole life. Stocks, because they have tangible value, can be traded over public exchanges, or they can be used as collateral to borrow money.

Examples

Equity for Cash: You purchase 100 shares at $27 per share, and place $2,700 plus trading fees into your account. You receive notice that the purchase has been completed. This is an equity investment, and you are a stockholder in the corporation.

Partway There: You buy an automobile for $10,000. You put down $3,000 and finance the difference of $7,000. Your equity is limited to your down payment of $3,000. You are the licensed owner, but the financed balance of $7,000 is not part of your equity.

The second broadly understood form is a *debt investment*, also called a debt instrument. This is a loan made by the investor to the company, government, or government agency, which promises to repay the loan plus interest, as a contractual obligation. The best-known form of debt instrument is the bond. Corporations, cities and states, the federal government, agencies, and subdivisions finance their operations and projects through bond issues, and investors in bonds are lenders, not stockholders.

When you own a bond, you also own a tangible value, not in stock but in a contractual right with the lender. The bond issuer promises to pay you interest and to repay the amount loaned by a specific date. Like stocks, bonds can be used as collateral to borrow money. They also rise and fall in value based on the interest rate a bond pays compared to current rates in today's market. In the event an issuer goes broke, bondholders are usually repaid before stockholders as part of their contract, so bonds have that advantage over stocks.

Examples

Lending Your Money: You purchase a bond currently valued at $9,700 from the U.S. government. Although you invest your funds in the same manner as a stockholder, you have become a bondholder; this does not provide any equity interest to you. You are a lender and you own a debt instrument.

Helping a Friend: A good friend wants to buy a car for $10,000, but has only $3,000 in cash. This friend asks you to lend him the balance of $7,000 and offers to pay interest to you. The $7,000 you contribute is a debt investment, and the interest you earn is income on that investment. When you act as lender, you have made a debt investment.

The third form of investing is less well-known. Equity and debt contain a tangible value that we can grasp and visualize. Part ownership in a company and the contractual right for repayment are basic features of equity and debt investments. Not only are these tangible, but they have a specific life span as well. Stock ownership lasts as long as you continue to own the stock and cannot be canceled unless the company goes broke; a bond has a contractual repayment schedule and ending date. The third form of investing does not contain these features; it disappears—expires—within a short period of time. You might hesitate at the idea of investing money in a product that evaporates and then ceases to have any value. In fact, there is no tangible value at all.

Key Point

Options are intangible and have a limited life span. The main advantage is that options allow you to control 100 shares of stock without having to buy those shares.

So we're talking about investing money in something with no tangible value, which will be absolutely worthless within a few months. To make this even more perplexing, imagine that the value of this intangible is certain to decline just because time passes by. To confuse the point even further, imagine that these attributes can be an advantage or a disadvantage, depending on how you decide to use these products.

These are some of the features of options. Taken alone (and out of context), these attributes certainly do not make this market seem very appealing. These attributes—lack of tangible value, worthlessness in the short term, and decline in value itself—make options seem far too risky

Valuable Resource
To find a worthwhile summary of risk complete with disclosures about the options market, download a copy of the industry prospectus, Characteristics and Risks of Standardized Options at **www.optionsclearing.com/about/publications/publication-listing.jsp.**

for most people. But there are good reasons for you to read on. Not all methods of investing in options are as risky as they might seem; some are quite conservative because the features just mentioned can work to your advantage. In whatever way you might use options, the many strategies that can be applied make options one of the more interesting avenues for investors. The more you study options, the more you realize that they are flexible; they can be used in numerous situations and to create numerous opportunities; and, most intriguing of all, they can be either exceptionally risky or downright conservative.

Key Point

Option strategies range from high risk to extremely conservative. The risk features on one end of the spectrum work to your advantage on the other. Options provide you with a rich variety of choices.

An *option* is a contract that provides you with the right to execute a stock transaction—that is, to buy or sell 100 shares of stock. (Each option always refers to a 100-share unit.) This right includes a specific stock and a specific fixed price per share that remains fixed until a specific date in the future. When you have an open option position, you do not have any equity in the stock, and neither do you have any debt position. You have only a contractual right to buy or to sell 100 shares of the stock at the fixed price.

Since you can always buy or sell 100 shares at the current market price, you might ask: "Why do I need to purchase an option to gain that right?" The answer is that the option fixes the price of stock, and this is the key to an option's value. Stock prices may rise or fall, at times significantly. Price movement of the stock is unpredictable, which makes stock market investing interesting and also defines the risk to the market itself. As an option owner, the stock price you can apply to buy or sell 100 shares is frozen for as long as the option remains in effect. So no matter how much price movement takes place, your price is fixed should you decide to purchase or sell 100 shares of that stock. Ultimately, an option's value is going to be determined by a comparison between the fixed price and the stock's current market price.

A few important restrictions come with options:

- The right to buy or to sell stock at the fixed price is never indefinite; in fact, time is the most critical factor because the option exists for a specific time only.

  When the deadline has passed, the option becomes worthless and ceases to exist. Because of this, the option's value is going to fall as the deadline approaches, and in a predictable manner.

- Each option also applies only to one specific stock and cannot be transferred.

- Each option applies to exactly 100 shares of stock, no more and no less.

Stock transactions commonly occur in blocks divisible by 100, called a *round lot*, which has become a standard trading unit on the public exchanges. In the market, you have the right to buy or sell an unlimited number of shares, assuming that they are available for sale and that you are willing to pay the seller's price. However, if you buy fewer than 100 shares in a single transaction, you will be charged a higher trading fee. An odd-numbered grouping of shares is called an *odd lot*.

So each option applies to 100 shares, conforming to the commonly traded lot, whether you are operating as a buyer or as a seller. There are two types of options. First is the *call*, which grants its owner the right to buy 100 shares of stock in a company. When you buy a call, it is as though the seller is saying to you, "I will allow you to buy 100 shares of this company's stock, at a specified price, at any time between now and a specified date in the future. For that privilege, I expect you to pay me the current call's price."

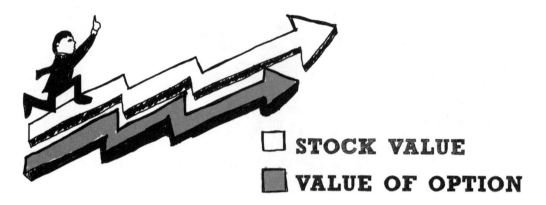

☐ **STOCK VALUE**

◼ **VALUE OF OPTION**

Each option's value changes according to changes in the price of the stock. If the stock's value rises, the value of the call option will follow suit and rise as well. And if the stock's market price falls, the call option will react in the same manner. When an investor buys a call and the stock's market value rises after the purchase, the investor profits because the call becomes more valuable. The value of an option actually is quite predictable—it is affected by the passage of time as well as by the ever-changing value of the stock.

ROUND LOT

ODD LOT

100 SHARES

72 SHARES

Key Point

Changes in the stock's value affect the value of the option directly, because while the stock's market price changes, the option's specified price per share remains the same. The changes in value are predictable; option valuation is no mystery.

The second type of option is the *put*. This is the opposite of a call in the sense that it grants a selling right instead of a purchasing right. The owner of a put contract has the right to sell 100 shares of stock. When you buy a put, it is as though the seller were saying to you, "I will allow you to sell me 100 shares of a specific company's stock, at a specified price per share, at any time between now and a specific date in the future. For that privilege, I expect you to pay me the current put's price."

The attributes of calls and puts can be clarified by remembering that either option can be bought or sold. This means there are four possible permutations to option transactions:

1. Buy a call (buy the right to buy 100 shares).
2. Sell a call (sell to someone else the right to buy 100 shares from you).
3. Buy a put (buy the right to sell 100 shares).
4. Sell a put (sell to someone else the right to sell 100 shares to you).

Another way to keep the distinction clear is to remember these qualifications: A call buyer believes and hopes that the stock's value will rise, but a put buyer is looking for the price per share to fall. If the belief is right in either case, then a profit may occur.

The opposite is true for sellers of options. A call seller hopes that the stock price will remain the same or fall, and a put seller hopes the price of the stock will rise. (The seller profits if the option's value falls—more on this later.)

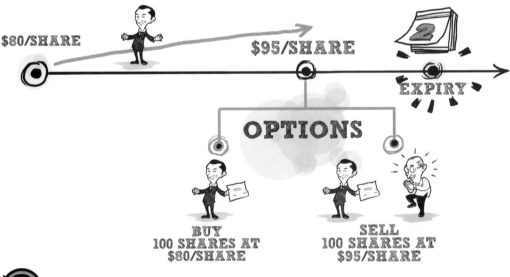

Key Point

Option buyers can profit whether the market rises or falls; the trick is knowing ahead of time which direction the market will take.

If an option buyer—dealing either in calls or in puts—is correct in predicting the price movement in the stock's market value, then the action of buying the option will be profitable. *Market value* is the price value agreed on by both buyer and seller, and is the common determining factor in the auction marketplace. However, when it comes to options, you have an additional obstacle besides estimating the direction of price movement: The change has to take place before the deadline that is attached to every option. You might be correct about a stock's long-term prospects, and as a stockholder you have the luxury of being able to wait out long-term change. However, this luxury is not available to option buyers. This is the critical point. Options are finite and, unlike stocks, they cease to exist and lose all their value within a relatively short period of time—within a few months for every *listed option*. (Long-term options last up to three years; more on these later.) Because of this daunting limitation to options trading, time is one important factor in determining whether an option buyer is able to earn a profit.

Key Point

It is not enough to accurately predict the direction of a stock's price movement. For option buyers, that movement has to occur quickly enough for that profit to materialize while the option still exists.

Why does the option's market value change when the stock's price moves up or down? First of all, the option is an intangible right, a contract lacking the kind of value associated, for example, with shares of stock. The option is an agreement relating to 100 shares of a specific stock and to a specific price per share. Consequently, if the buyer's timing is poor—meaning the stock's movement doesn't occur or is not substantial enough by the deadline—then the buyer will not realize a profit.

When you buy a call, it is as though you are saying, "I am willing to pay the price being asked to acquire a contractual right. That right provides that I *may* buy 100 shares of stock at the specified fixed price per share, and this right exists to buy those shares at any time between my option purchase date and the specified deadline." If the stock's market price rises above the fixed price indicated in the option agreement, the call becomes more valuable. Imagine that you buy a call option granting you the right to buy 100 shares at the price of $80 per share. Before the deadline, though, the stock's market price rises to $95 per share. As the owner of a call option, you have the right to buy 100 shares at $80, or 15 points below the *current market value*. This is the purchaser's advantage in the scenario described, when market value exceeds the fixed contractual price indicated in the call's contract. In that instance, you as buyer would have the right to buy 100 shares 15 points below current market value. You own the right, but you are not obligated to follow through. For example, if your call granted you the right to buy 100 shares at $80 per share but the stock's market price fell to $70, you would not have to buy shares at the fixed price of $80; you could elect to take no action.

The same scenario applies to buying puts, but with the stock moving in the opposite direction. When you buy a put, it is as though you are saying, "I am willing to pay the asked price to buy a contractual right. That right provides that I may sell 100 shares of the specified stock at the indicated price per share, at any time between my option purchase date and the specified deadline." If the stock's price falls below that level, you will be able to sell 100 shares *above* current market value. For example, let's say that you buy a put option providing you with the right to sell

100 shares at $80 per share. Before the deadline, the stock's market value falls to $70 per share. As the owner of a put, you have the right to sell 100 shares at the fixed price of $80, which is $10 per share above the current market value. You own the right but you are not obligated. For example, if your put granted you the right to sell 100 shares at $70 but the stock's market price rose to $85 per

contract

A single option, the agreement providing the buyer with the terms that option grants. Those terms include identification of the stock, the cost of the option, the date the option will expire, and the fixed price per share of the stock to be bought or sold under the rights of the option.

share, you would not be required to sell at the fixed price. You could sell at the higher market price, which would be more profitable. The potential advantage to option buyers is found in the contractual rights that they acquire. These rights are central to the nature of options, and each option bought or sold is referred to as a *contract*.

THE CALL OPTION

A call is the right to buy 100 shares of stock at a fixed price per share, at any time between the purchase of the call and the specified future deadline. This time is limited. As a call *buyer*, you acquire the right, and as a call *seller*, you grant the right of the option to someone else. (See Figure 1.1.)

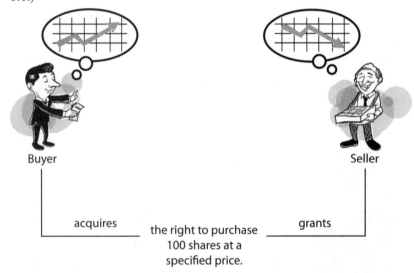

Buyer   Seller

acquires   the right to purchase 100 shares at a specified price.   grants

Figure 1.1 The Call Option

Let's walk through an illustration and apply both buying and selling as they relate to the call option.

- *Buyer of a call*: When you buy a call, you hope that the stock will rise in value, because that will result in a corresponding increase in value for the call. This will create higher market value in the call, which can be sold and closed at a profit; or the stock can be bought at a fixed price lower than the current market value.
- *Seller of a call*: When you sell a call, you hope that the stock will fall in value, because that will result in a corresponding de-

crease in value for the call. This will create lower market value for the call, which can then be purchased and closed at a profit; or the stock can be sold to the buyer at a price above current market value. The order is the reverse from the better-known buyer's position. The call seller will first sell and then, later on, will close the transaction with a buy order. (More information on selling calls is presented in Chapter 5.)

The backwards sequence used by call sellers is often difficult to grasp for anyone accustomed to the more traditional buy-hold-sell pattern. The seller's approach is to sell-hold-buy. Remembering that time is running for every option contract, the seller, by reversing the sequence, has a distinct advantage over the buyer. Time is on the seller's side.

Key Point

Option sellers reverse the sequence by selling first and buying later. This strategy has many advantages, especially considering the restriction of time unique to the option contract. Time benefits the seller.

Prices of listed options—those traded publicly on exchanges like the New York, Chicago, and Philadelphia stock exchanges—are established strictly through *supply and demand*. Those are the forces that dictate whether market prices rise or fall for stocks. As more buyers want stocks, prices are driven upward by their demand; and as more sellers want to sell shares of stock, prices decline due to increased supply. The supply and demand for stocks, in turn, affect the market value of options. The option itself has no direct fundamental value or underlying financial reasons for rising or falling; its market value is a by-product of the fundamental and technical changes in the stock.

Key Point

The market forces affecting the value of stocks in turn affect market values of options. The option itself has no actual fundamental value; its market value is formulated based on the stock's fundamentals.

The orderly process of buying and selling stocks, which establishes stock price values, takes place on the exchanges through trading available to the general public. This overall public trading activity, in which prices are being established through ever-changing supply and demand, is called the *auction market*, because value is not controlled by any forces other than the market itself. These forces include economic news and perceptions, earnings of listed companies, news and events affecting products and services, competitive forces, and Wall Street events, both positive and negative. Individual stock prices also rise or fall based on index motion.

Stocks issued by corporations are limited in number, but the exchanges will allow investors to buy or sell as many options as they want. The *number* of active options is unlimited. However, the values in option contracts respond directly to changes in the stock's value. The two primary factors affecting an option's value are time and the market value of the stock.

Key Point

Option value is affected by movement in the price of the stock and by the passage of time. Supply and demand affect option valuation only indirectly.

STOCK EXCHANGE
AUCTION MARKET

NEWS
PERCEPTION
EARNINGS
WALLSTREET EVENTS

The owner of a call enjoys an important benefit in the auction market. There is always a *ready market* for the option at the current market price. That means that the owner of an option never has a problem selling that option.

This feature is of critical importance. For example, if there were constantly more buyers than sellers of options, then market value would be distorted beyond reason. To some degree, distortions do occur on the basis of rumor or speculation, usually in the short term. But by and large, option values are directly formulated on the basis of stock prices and time until the option will cease to exist. If buyers had to scramble to find a limited number of willing sellers, the market would not work efficiently. Demand between buyers and sellers in options is rarely equal because options do not possess supply-and-demand features of their own. So the Options Clearing Corporation (OCC) acts as the seller to every buyer, and as the buyer to every seller.

ready market

A liquid market, one in which buyers can easily sell their holdings, or in which sellers can easily find buyers, at current market prices.

STOCK OPTIONS

TIME MARKET
VALUE OF STOCK

Valuable Resource
Learn more about the Options Clearing Corporation (OCC) at their website, **www.theocc.com**. This page includes current market information, resources for options trading, and a link to the options prospectus, "Characteristics and Risks of Standardized Options." The prospectus can also be viewed at the Chicago Board Options Exchange (CBOE) website, **www. cboe.com/Resources/intro.aspx.**

How Call Buying Works

When you buy a call, you are not required to buy the 100 shares of stock. You have the *right*, but not the obligation. In fact, the vast majority of call buyers do not actually buy 100 shares of stock. Most buyers are speculating on the price movement of the stock, hoping to sell their options at a profit rather than buy 100 shares of stock. As a buyer, you have until the *expiration date* to decide what action to take, if any. You have several choices, and the best one to make depends entirely on what happens to the market price of the *underlying stock*, and on how much time remains in the option period.

Using calls to illustrate, there are three scenarios relating to the price of the underlying stock, and several choices for action within each.

1. *The market value of the underlying stock rises.* In the event of an increase in the price of the underlying stock, you may take one of two actions. First, you may exercise the call and buy the 100 shares of stock below current market value. Second, if you do not want to own 100 shares of that stock, you may sell the option for a profit.

   Every option has a fixed value at which exercise takes place. Whenever an option is exercised, the purchase price of 100 shares of stock takes place at that fixed price, which is called the *striking price* of the option. Striking price is expressed as a numerical equivalent of the dollar price per share, without dollar signs. The striking price is normally divisible by 5, as options are established with striking prices at five-dollar price intervals for stocks selling between $30 and $200 per share. Stocks selling under $30 have options trading at 2.5-point intervals; and stocks trading above $200 per share have options trading at $10 intervals. When a stock splits, new striking price levels may also be introduced. For example, if a stock is split 2-for-1 and it has a current option at 35, the post-split levels would be adjusted to 17. (In cases of splits, the number of shares and options are adjusted so that the ratio of one option per 100 shares of stock remains constant. In a 2-for-1 split, 100 shares become 200 shares at half the value; and each outstanding option becomes two options worth half the pre-split value.)

Example

Profitable Decisions: You decided two months ago to buy a call. You paid the option price of $200, which entitled you to buy 100 shares of a particular stock at $55 per share. The striking price is 55. The option will expire later this month. The stock currently is selling for $60 per share, and the option's current value is 6 ($600). You have a choice to make: You may exercise the call and buy 100 shares at the contractual price of $55 per share, which is $5 per share below current market value; or you may sell the call and realize a profit of $400 on the investment, consisting of current market value of the option of $600, less the original price of $200. (This example does not include an adjustment for trading costs, so in applying this and other examples, remember that it will cost you a fee each time you enter an option transaction and each time you leave one. This should be factored into any calculation of profit or loss on an option trade.)

2. *The market value of the underlying stock does not change.* It often happens that within the life span of an option, the stock's market value does not change, or changes are too insignificant to create the profit scenario you hope for when you buy calls. You have two alternatives in this situation. First, you may sell the call at a loss before its expiration date (after which the call becomes worthless). Second, you may hold on to the option, hoping that the stock's market value will rise before expiration, which would create a rise in the call's value as well, at the last minute. The first choice, selling at a loss, is advisable when it appears there is no hope of a last-minute surge in the stock's market value. Taking some money out and reducing your loss may be wiser than waiting for the option to lose even more

value. Remember, after expiration date, the option is worthless. An option is a *wasting asset*, because it is designed to lose all its value after expiration. By its limited life attribute, it is expected to decline in value as time passes. If the market value of the stock remains at or below the striking price all the way to expiration, then the *premium value*—the current market value of the option—will be much less near expiration than at the time you purchased it, even if the stock's market value remains the same. The difference reflects the value of time itself. The longer the time until expiration, the more opportunity there is for the stock (and the option) to change in value.

Key Point

In setting standards for yourself to determine when or if to take profits in an option, be sure to factor in the cost of the transaction. Brokerage fees and charges vary widely, so shop around for the best option deal based on the volume of trading you undertake.

Example

Best Laid Plans: You purchased a call a few months ago "at 5." (This means you paid a premium of $500). You hoped that the underlying stock would increase in market value, causing the option also to rise in value. The call will expire later this month, but contrary to your expectations, the stock's price has not changed. The option's value has declined to $100. You have the choice of selling it now and taking a $400 loss, or you may hold the option, hoping for a last-minute increase in the stock's value. Either way, you will need to sell the option before expiration, after which it will become worthless.

Key Point

The options market is characterized by a series of choices, some more difficult than others. It requires discipline to apply a formula so that you make the best decision given the circumstances, rather than acting on impulse. That is the key to succeeding with options.

3. *The market value of the underlying stock falls.* As the underlying stock's market value falls, the value of all related calls will fall as well. The value of the option is always related to the value of the underlying stock. If the stock's market price falls significantly, your call will show very little in the way of market value. You may sell and accept the loss or, if the option is worth nearly nothing, you may simply allow it to expire and take a full loss on the transaction.

This example demonstrates that buying calls is risky. The last-minute rescue of an option by a sudden increase in the value of the underlying stock can and does happen, but usually it does not. The limited life of the option works against the call buyer, so that the entire amount invested could be lost. The most significant advantage in speculating in calls is that instead of losing a larger sum in buying 100 shares of stock, the loss is limited to the relatively small premium value. At the same time, you could profit significantly as a call buyer because less money is at risk. The stockholder, in comparison, has the advantage of being able to hold stock indefinitely, without having to worry about expiration dates. For stockholders, patience is always possible, and it might take many months or even years for growth in value to occur. The stockholder is under no pressure to act because stock does not expire as options do.

Example

Dashed Hopes: You bought a call four months ago and paid 3 (a premium of $300). You were hoping that the stock's market value would rise, also causing a rise in the value of the call. Instead, the stock's market value fell, and the option followed suit. It is now worth only 1 ($100). You have a choice: You may sell the call for 1 and accept a loss of $200, or you may hold on to the call until near expiration. The stock could rise in value at the last minute, which has been known to happen. However, by continuing to hold the call, you risk further deterioration in the call premium value. If you wait until expiration occurs, the call will be worthless.

Example

Limiting Risks: You bought a call last month for 1 (premium of $100). The current price of the stock is $80 per share. For your $100 investment, you have a degree of control over 100 shares, without having to invest $8,000. Your risk is limited to the $100 investment; if the stock's market value falls, you cannot lose more than the $100, no matter what. In comparison, if you paid $8,000 to acquire 100 shares of stock, you could afford to wait indefinitely for a profit to appear, but you would have to tie up $8,000. You could also lose much more; if the stock's market value falls to $50 per share, your investment will have lost $3,000 in market value.

Key Point

For anyone speculating over the short term, option buying is an excellent method of controlling large blocks of stock with minor commitments of capital.

In some respects, the preceding example defines the difference between investing and speculating. The very idea of investing usually indicates a long-term mentality and perspective. Because stock does not expire, investors enjoy the luxury of being able to wait out short-term market conditions, hoping that over several years that company's fortunes will lead to profits—not to mention continuing dividends and ever-higher market value for the stock. There is no denying that stockholders enjoy clear advantages over option buyers. They can wait indefinitely for the market to go their way. They earn dividend income. And stock can be used as collateral for buying or financing other assets. Speculators, in comparison, risk losing their entire investment, while also being exposed to the opportunity for spectacular gains. Rather than considering one method as being better than the other, think of options as yet another way to use investment capital. Option buyers know that their risk/reward scenario is characterized by the ever-looming expiration date. To understand how the speculative nature of call buying affects you, consider the following two examples.

Key Point

The limited life of options defines the risk/reward scenario, and option players recognize this as part of their strategy. The risk is accepted because the opportunity is there, too.

Example

Rising Hopes and Prices: You buy an 80 call for 2 ($200), which provides you with the right to buy 100 shares of stock for $80 per share. If the stock's value rises above $80, your call will rise in value dollar for dollar along with the stock. So if the stock goes up $4 per share to $84, the option will also rise 4 points, or $400 in value. You would earn a profit of $200 if you were to sell the call at that point (4 points of value less the purchase price of 2). That would be the same amount of profit you would realize by purchasing 100 shares of stock at $8,000 and selling those shares for $8,200. (Again, this example does not take into account any brokerage and trading costs. Chances are that fees for the stock trade would be higher than for an option trade because more money is being exchanged.)

Example

Failing Expectations: You buy an 80 call for 2 ($200), which gives you the right to buy 100 shares of stock at $80 per share. By the call's expiration date, the stock has fallen to $68 per share. You lose the entire $200 investment as the call becomes worthless. However, if you had purchased 100 shares of stock and paid $8,000, your loss at this point would be $1,200 ($80 per share at purchase, less current market value of $68 per share). Your choice, then, would be to sell the stock and take the loss or continue to keep your capital tied up, hoping its value will eventually rebound. Compared to buying stock directly, the option risks are limited. Stockholders can wait out a temporary drop in price, even indefinitely. However, the stockholder has no way of knowing when the stock's price will rebound, or even whether it ever will do so. As an option buyer, you are at risk for only a few months at the most. One of the risks in buying stock is the *lost opportunity risk*—capital is committed in a loss situation while other opportunities come and go.

In situations where an investment in stock loses value, stockholders can wait for a rebound. During that time, they are entitled to continue receiving dividends, so their investment is not entirely in limbo. If you are seeking long-term gains, then a temporary drop in market value is not catastrophic as long as you continue to believe that the company remains a viable long-term "hold" candidate; market fluctuations might even be expected. Some investors would see such a drop as a buying opportunity and pick up even more shares. The effect of this move is to lower the overall basis in the stock, so that a rebound creates even greater returns later on.

Key Point

A long-term investor can hold stock indefinitely and does not have to worry about expiration. Option buyers have to worry continually about expiration dates.

The advantage in buying calls is that you are not required to tie up a large sum of capital or to keep it at risk for a long time. Yet you are able to control 100 shares of stock for each option purchased as though you had bought those shares outright. Losses are limited to the amount of premium you pay.

The Long-Term Call Option

The greatest inhibiting factor in evaluating calls is time. As a call buyer, you need to continually be aware that expiration forces a decision point; profits have to materialize before expiration, or the call buyer loses money.

The listed option has a life span of only a few months, normally eight or so; the price movement of the stock has to be substantial enough to overcome this time factor. For many buyers, the short life span of calls makes them impractical as a speculative position. To overcome this problem, call buyers may also consider using long-term options. These work just like listed options in every respect, with one exception: Their life span lasts up to three years.

A long-term equity anticipation security (LEAPS) is a long-term option that can be used to solve the problem of time. Unlike the relatively short-lived listed option, LEAPS can be used to expand many strategies that would otherwise be impractical, given the time factor.

The long-term option, because of its extended life, can be employed for some strategies that are not practical with shorter-expiration contracts. LEAPS can be used as an alternative to buying stock and placing large sums of capital at risk. This could change the way that you invest in volatile market conditions. They can also be used to protect paper profits over a period of time, in combination with other strategies, and for speculative or conservative strategies. The choice of using listed options or LEAPS options expands the range of strategies and makes the entire field of options far more flexible; options traders can look beyond the eight-month range that is typical for listed options and achieve far more with a greater amount of time in play.

lost opportunity risk (stock)

The risk stockholders experience in tying up capital over the long term, causing lost opportunities that could be taken if capital were available.

Valuable Resource
To read more about how LEAPS options work, check the tutorial at the Options Industry Council (OIC): **www.optionseducation.org/basics/leaps/leaps_2.jsp.**

In considering calls and reviewing the broad range of risk levels, you can consider both short-term and long-term options in developing investment standards. Throughout the remainder of this book, many examples employ listed options as well as LEAPS options to illustrate how strategies can be used in a number of different ways.

Investment Standards for Call Buyers

Whether using shorter-term listed options or LEAPS calls, you need to not only be aware of risk levels, but also to establish a clear investment standard for yourself. This means much more than merely taking the advice of a stockbroker or financial planner; it means considering a range of ideas and choosing standards that fit well for you, individually.

People who work in the stock market—including brokers who help investors to decide what to buy and sell—regularly offer advice on stocks. If a stockbroker, analyst, or financial planner is qualified, he or she may also offer advice on trading in options. Three important points should be kept in mind when working with a broker, especially where option buying is involved.

1. *You need to develop your own expertise.* The broker might not know as much about the market as you do. Just because someone has a license does not mean that he or she is an expert on all types of investments. In fact, due to the nature of the options market, you may want to become proficient at making your own options-related decisions. In this case, you may wish to continue employing outside help for stock-related decisions, but maintain direct control over options trading.

2. *You cannot expect on-the-job training as an options investor.* Don't expect a broker to train you. Remember, brokers earn their living on commissions and placement of orders. That means their primary motive is to get clients to buy and to sell. Here again, you may depend on a broker's expertise when it comes to stocks, but you should not assume that the same broker is knowledgeable about options strategies or risks.

3. *There are no guarantees.* Risk is found everywhere and in all markets. While it is true that call buying involves specific risk, this does not mean that buying stock is safe

⌐ ⌐ ı risk levels for
⌐ ⌐ ɪould be aware of
⌐ ⌐ ⌐ ⌐ ɪisk levels; options
⌐ ⌐ ⌐ ⌐ to separate stock and
⌐ ⌐ ⌐ ⌐ think that there are
any risk-free investments using stocks, options, or the two together. The fact is, once you become comfortable with options
trading, you are going to be less likely to depend on a broker
for any advice. Options traders tend to think for themselves,
and come to realize that they can operate without the services
that come with paying full-price commissions.

Key Point

Anyone who wants to be involved with options will eventually
realize that a broker's advice is unnecessary and could even
get in the way of an efficient trading program.

Some traders continue using brokers due to personal loyalty or a track
record of exceptional advice. Whether you are seeking a broker or using
one already, that broker should not give the same recommendations to
everyone; advice should be matched to specific risk levels and experience.
Brokers are required by law to ensure that you are qualified to invest in
options. That means that you should have at least a minimal understanding of market risks, procedures, and terminology, and that you understand the risks associated with options. Brokers are required to apply a
rule called *know your customer*. The brokerage firm has to ask you to complete a form that documents your knowledge or experience with options;
firms also give out *a prospectus*, which is a document explaining all of the
risks of option investing.

The investment standard for buying calls includes the requirement that
you know how the market works and that you invest only funds that you
can afford to have at risk. Beyond that, you have every right to decide for
yourself how much risk you want to take. Ultimately, you are responsible
for your own profits and losses in the market. The role of the broker is to
document the fact that the right questions were asked before your money
was taken and placed into the option. One of the most common mistakes
made, especially by inexperienced investors, is to believe that brokers
are responsible for providing guidance. They are not. However, they are
required to make sure you know what you're doing before you proceed.

How Call Selling Works

Buying calls is similar to buying stock, at least regarding the sequence of events. You invest money and, after some time has passed, you make the decision to sell. The transaction takes place in a predictable order. Call selling doesn't work that way. A seller begins by selling a call, and later on buys the same call to close out the transaction.

Many people have trouble grasping the idea of selling before buying. A common reaction is, "Are you sure? Is that legal?" or "How can you sell something that you don't own?" It is legal, and you can sell something before you buy it. This is done all the time in the stock market through a strategy known *as short selling*. An investor sells stock that he or she does not own, and later places a buy order, which closes the position.

The same technique is used in the options market and is far less complicated than selling stock short. Because options have no tangible value, becoming an option seller is fairly easy. A call seller grants the right to someone else—a buyer—to buy 100 shares of stock, at a fixed price per share and by a specified expiration date. For granting this right, the call seller is paid a premium. As a call seller, you are paid for the sale but you must also be willing to deliver 100 shares of stock if the call buyer exercises the option. This strategy, the exact opposite of buying calls, has a different array of risks than those experienced by the call buyer. The greatest risk is that the option you sell could be exercised, and you would be required to sell 100 shares of stock far below the current market value.

When you operate as an option buyer, the decision to exercise or not is entirely up to you. But as a seller, that decision is always made by someone else. As an option seller, you can make or lose money in three different ways:

1. *The market value of the underlying stock rises.* In this instance, the value of the call rises as well. For a buyer, this is good news. But for the seller, the opposite is true. If the buyer exercises the call, the 100 shares of stock have to be delivered by the option seller. In practice, this means you are required to pay the difference between the option's striking price and the stock's current market value. As a seller, this means you lose money. Remember, the option will be exercised only if the stock's current market value is higher than the striking price of the option.

Example

Called Away: You sell a call with a striking price of 40 per share. You happen to own 100 shares of the underlying stock, so you consider your risks to be minimal in selling a call. (If the buyer exercises the call, you already own the shares and would be willing to sell them at the striking price.) In addition, the call is worth $200, and that amount is paid to you for selling the call. One month later, the stock's market value has risen to $46 per share and the buyer exercises the call. You are obligated to deliver the 100 shares of stock at $40 per share. This is $6 per share below current market value. Although you received a premium of $200 for selling the call, you lose the increased market value in the stock, which is $600. Your net loss in this case is $400.

The loss in this example would be viewed based on your original cost of the stock. A call seller selects striking prices based on the original cost of the stock. So if you originally paid $42 per share for the stock and it is called away at $40, you break even before trading costs. (A $2-per-share loss is offset by the premium you were paid for selling the call.) However, if your original cost of the stock was $35 per share, your overall net profit would be $700—a $500 capital gain on the stock plus $200 in option premium.

Example

More Risk, More Loss: Given the same conditions as the preceding example, let's now assume that you did not own 100 shares of stock. What happens if the option is exercised? In this case, you are still required to deliver 100 shares at $40 per share. Current market value is $46, so you are required to buy the shares at that price and then sell them at $40, a net loss of $400. ($600 difference in values, less $200 you received for selling the call.) In practice, you would be required to pay the difference rather than physically buying and then selling 100 shares.

Key Point

Call sellers have much less risk when they already own their 100 shares. They can select calls in such a way that in the event of exercise, the stock investment will still be profitable.

The difference between these two examples is that in the first case, you owned the shares and could deliver them if the option were exercised. There is even the possibility that you originally purchased those shares below the $40 per share value. So in effect, you exchanged potential gain in the stock for the value of the call premium you received. In the second example, it is all loss because you have to buy the shares at current market value and sell them for less.

When the call is exercised, it doesn't always translate to a loss. If you received enough premium for selling the call, you could still make a profit.

Example

The LEAPS Call Alternative: You sold a LEAPS call with 30 months until expiration. Because that is a long time away, you were paid a much higher premium than you would have received for selling a shorter-term listed option. You were paid 12 ($1,200) when you sold the call. A few months later, the stock is four points higher than the striking price, and your broker notifies you that your option has been called. You are required to pay the difference between current market value and striking price, which is 400. The net effect is a profit of $800 (before considering trading costs). When using a LEAPS call in a short sale, a higher premium grants you more cushion.

2. The market value of the stock does not change. In the case where the stock's value remains at or near the price level when the call was sold, the value of the call will decline over time. Remember, the call is a wasting asset. While that is a problem for the call buyer, it is a great advantage for the call seller. Time works against the buyer, but it works for the call seller. You have the right to close out your short call at any time before expiration date. So you may sell a call and hope that it declines in value; and then buy it to close the position at a lower premium, with the difference representing your profit.

Example

Profiting from Inertia: You sell a call for a premium of 4 ($400). Two months later, the stock's market value is about the same as it was when you sold the call. The option's premium value has fallen to 1 ($100). You cancel your position by buying the call at 1, realizing a profit of $300.

3. The market value of the stock falls. In this case, the option will also fall in value. This provides you with an advantage as a call seller. Remember, you are paid a premium at the time you sell the call. You want to close out your position at a later date, or wait for the call to expire worthless. You may do either in this case. Because time works against the buyer, it would take a considerable change in the stock's market value to change your profitable position in the sold option.

Example

Profits from Falling Prices: You sell a LEAPS call and receive a premium of 12 ($1,200). The stock's market value later falls far below the striking price of the option and, in your opinion, a recovery is not likely. As long as the market value of the stock is at or below the striking price at expiration, the option will not be exercised. By allowing the option to expire in this situation, the entire $1,200 you received is profit.

Remember three key points as a call seller. First, the transaction takes place in reverse order, with sale occurring before the purchase. Second, when you sell a call, you are paid a premium; in comparison, a call buyer pays the premium at the point of purchase. Third, what is good news for the buyer is bad news for the seller, and vice versa.

When you sell a call option, you are a short seller and that places you into what is called a *short position*. The sale is the opening transaction, and it can be closed in one of two ways. First, a buy order can be entered, and that closes out the position. Second, you may wait until expiration, after which the option ceases to exist and the position closes automatically. In comparison, the better-known "buy first, sell later" approach is called a *long position*. The long position is also closed in one of two ways. Either the buyer enters a sell order, closing the position, or the option expires worthless, so that the buyer loses the entire premium value.

THE PUT OPTION

A put is the opposite of a call. It is a contract granting the right to sell 100 shares of stock at a fixed price per share and by a specified expiration date in the future. As a put buyer, you acquire the right to sell 100 shares of stock; and as a put seller, you grant that right to the buyer. (See Figure 1.2.)

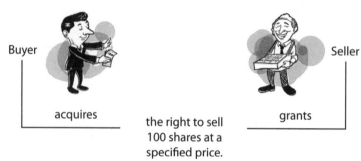

Buyer   acquires   the right to sell 100 shares at a specified price.   grants   Seller

Figure 1.2 The Put Option

Buying and Selling Puts

As a buyer of a put, you hope the underlying stock's value will fall. A put is the opposite of a call and so it acts in the opposite manner as the stock's market value changes. If the stock's market value falls, the put's value rises; and if the stock's market value rises, then the put's value falls. There are three possible outcomes when you buy puts.

1. *The market value of the stock rises.* In this case, the put's value falls in response. Thus, you may sell the put for a price below the price you paid and take a loss; or you may hold on to the put, hoping that the stock's market value will fall before the expiration date.

Example

Turning it Upside Down: You bought a put two months ago, paying a premium of 2 ($200). You expected the stock's market price to fall, in which case the value of the put would have risen. Instead, the stock's market value rose, so the put's value fell. It is now worth only 0.25, or $25. You have a choice: Sell the put and take a $175 loss, or hold on to the put, hoping the stock will fall before the expiration date. If you hold the put beyond expiration, it will be worthless and your loss will be the full $200.

This example demonstrates the need to assess risks. For example, with the put currently worth only $25—nearly nothing—there is very little value remaining, so you might consider it too late to cut your losses in this case. Considering that there is only $25 at stake, it might be worth the long shot of holding the put until expiration. If the stock's price does fall between now and then, you stand the chance of recovering your investment and, perhaps, even earning a profit.

Key Point

Option traders constantly calculate risk and reward, and often make decisions based not on how they hoped prices would change, but on how an unexpected change has affected their position.

2. *The market value of the stock does not change.* If the stock does not move significantly enough to alter the value of the put, then the put's value will still fall. The put, like the call, is a wasting asset; so the more time that passes and the closer the expiration date becomes, the less value will remain in the put. In this situation, you may sell the put and accept a loss, or hold on to it, hoping that the stock's market price will fall before the put's expiration.

Example

Choosing Between Bad and Worse: You bought a LEAPS put several months ago and paid a premium of 7 ($700). You had expected the stock's market value to fall, in which case the put's value would have risen. Expiration comes up later this month. Unfortunately, the stock's market value is about the same as it was when you bought the LEAPS put, but that put is now worth only $100. Your choices: Sell the put for $100 and accept the $600 loss, or hold on to the put on the chance that the stock's value will fall before expiration.

The choice comes down to a matter of timing and an awareness of how much price change is required to produce a breakeven point or a profit. In the preceding example, the stock would have to fall at least seven points below the put's striking price just to create a breakeven outcome (before trading costs). In this case, even utilizing a longer-term LEAPS put, the option profit simply did not materialize before expiration. If you have more time, your choice would be easier because you could defer your decision to either take a loss or just wait out the price movement of the stock. You can afford to adopt a wait-and-see attitude with a long time to go before expiration, which makes the LEAPS a more flexible choice than shorter-term listed options. The value of any option tends to fall slowly at first, and then more rapidly as expiration approaches.

3. The market value of the stock falls. In this case, the put's value will rise. You have three alternatives. First, you may hold the put in the hope that the stock's market value will decline even more, increasing your profit. Second, you may sell the put and take your profit now. Third, you may exercise the put and sell 100 shares of the underlying stock at the striking price. That price will be above current market value, so you will profit from exercise by selling at the higher striking price.

Example

Having It Both Ways: You own 100 shares of stock that you bought last year for $38 per share, and the price later rose above $40. You were worried about the threat of a falling market; however, you also wanted to hold on to your stock as a long-term investment. To protect yourself against the possibility of a price decline in your stock, you bought a put, paying a premium of 0.50, or $50. This guarantees you the right to sell 100 shares for $40 per share. Recently, the price of your stock fell to $33 per share. The value of the put increased to $750, offsetting your loss in the stock.

You can make a choice given the preceding example. You may sell the put and realize a profit of $700, which offsets the loss in the stock. This choice is appealing because you can take a profit in the put, but you continue to own the stock. So if the stock's price rebounds, you will benefit twice.

A second alternative is to exercise the put and sell the 100 shares at $40 per share (the striking price of the option), which is $7 per share above current market value (but only $2 per share above the price you paid originally for the stock). This choice could be appealing if you believe that circumstances have changed and that it was a mistake to buy the stock as a long-term investment. By getting out now with a profit instead of a loss, you recover your full investment even though the stock's market value has fallen. This alternative makes sense if and when you would prefer to get out of the stock position; with the put investment, you can make that choice profitably, even though the stock's market value has fallen.

A third choice is to hold off taking any immediate action. The put acts as a form of insurance to protect your investment in the stock against further price declines. That's because at this point, for every drop in the stock's price, the option's value will offset that drop, point for point. If the stock's value increases, the option's value will decline dollar for dollar. So the two positions offset one another. As long as you take action before the put's expiration, your risk is virtually eliminated.

Key Point

At times, inaction is the smartest choice. Depending on the circumstances, you could be better off patiently waiting out price movements until the day before expiration.

While you may buy puts believing the stock's market value will fall, or to protect your stock position, you may also sell puts. As a put seller, you grant someone else the right to sell 100 shares of stock to you at a fixed price. If the put is exercised, you will be required to buy 100 shares of the stock at the striking price, which would be above the market value of the stock. For taking this risk, you are paid a premium when you sell the put. Like the call seller, put sellers do not control the outcome of their position as much as buyers do, since it is the buyer who has the right to exercise at any time.

Example

Waiting It Out: Last month, you sold a put with a striking price of $50 per share. The premium was $250, which was paid to you at the time of the sale. Since then, the stock's market value has remained in a narrow range between $48 and $53 per share. Currently, the price is at $51. You do not expect the stock's price to fall below the striking price of 50. As long as the market value of the underlying stock remains at or above that level, the put will not be exercised. (The buyer will not exercise, meaning that you will not be required to buy 100 shares of stock.) If your prediction turns out to be correct, you can make a profit by selling the put once its value has declined.

Your risk in this example is that the stock's market price could decline below $50 per share before expiration, meaning that upon exercise you would be required to buy 100 shares at $50 per share. To avoid that risk, you have the right to cancel the position by buying the put at current market value. The closer you are to expiration (and as long as the stock's market value is above the striking price), the lower the market value of the put—and the greater your profit.

Put selling also makes sense if you believe that the striking price represents a fair price for the stock. In the worst case, you will be required to buy 100 shares at a price above current market value. If you are right, though, and the striking price is a fair price, then the stock's market value will eventually rebound to that price or above. In addition, to calculate the real loss on buying, overpriced stock has to be discounted for the premium you received.

Selling puts is a vastly different strategy from buying puts, because it places you on the opposite side of the transaction. The risk profile is different as well. If the put you sell is exercised, then you end up with overpriced stock, so you need to establish a logical standard for yourself if you sell puts. Never sell a put unless you are willing to acquire 100 shares of the underlying stock at the striking price.

One advantage for put sellers is that time works for you and against the buyer. As expiration approaches, the put loses value. However, if movement in the underlying stock is opposite the movement you expected, you could end up taking a loss or having to buy 100 shares of stock for each put you sell. Sudden and unexpected changes in the stock's market value can occur at any time. The more volatile a stock's price movement, the greater your risk as a seller. You might also notice as you observe the pricing of options that, due to higher risks, options on volatile stocks tend to hold higher premium values than those on more predictable, lower volatility issues.

Key Point

Option price behavior is directly affected by the underlying stock and its attributes. So volatile (higher risk) stocks demand higher option premiums and tend to experience faster, more severe price changes.

Put selling strategies can be more flexible when employing LEAPS. Because there is greater time to go until expiration, the LEAPS put seller has two advantages. First, the potential decline in stock price is limited in comparison to the potential rise in the case of using short calls; and second, the premium is likely to be higher than for shorter-term listed puts.

The potential decline in stock price is limited in two ways. First, the difference between the striking price and zero is a known quantity. Second and more realistically, the price of stock is not likely to fall below *tangible book value* per share. So risks in short selling of puts is limited. You will recall that short selling of calls is far riskier because, in theory at least, a stock's price could rise indefinitely.

The second factor—the LEAPS premium—makes put selling practical due to the cushion that premium provides. However, the larger premium also reflects a longer time period that LEAPS put sellers remain at risk; so offsetting the advantage, there is also the disadvantage of having to wait longer for those profits to materialize.

Example

The Premium Cushion: You believe that a particular stock is likely to rise in value. It is currently selling at $41 per share. The 30-month LEAPS puts at a striking price of 40 are available at 9 ($900). You sell a LEAPS put and receive payment of $900.

If the stock's value falls as low as $31 per share, you have downside protection (before trading costs are calculated) due to the nine points you were paid in premium. However, even if that put were to be exercised, you consider $40 per share a reasonable price to pay for the stock. You believe its long-term prospects are strong, so you would not mind picking up shares at that price level. Considering the payment of $900 for the LEAPS put, *your net basis* in stock upon exercise would be only $31 per share.

OPTION VALUATION

Option values change in direct proportion to the changing market value of the underlying stock. Every option is associated specifically with the stock of a single corporation and cannot be interchanged with others. How you fare in your option positions depends on how the stock's value changes in the immediate future.

The question of selecting stocks is more involved and complex than the method of picking an option. For options, the selection has to do with risk assessment, current value, time until expiration, and your own risk tolerance level; in addition, numerous strategies you may employ will affect the ultimate decision. But option selection is formulated predictably. In comparison, stock selection involves no precise formula that works in every case. Price movement in the stock itself cannot be known in advance, whereas the reaction of option premium value is completely predictable, based on the way the stock's price changes.

The selection of a stock is the critical decision point that determines whether you will succeed with options. This observation applies for buying or selling stock, and also applies when you never intend to own the stock at all but only want to deal with options themselves. It is a mistake to pick options based only on current value and time, hoping to succeed, without also thinking about the particulars of the stock—volatility, relation to striking price of the option, and much more. Of course, to some degree, the features of the option can be used to calculate likely outcomes, but that is only a part of the whole picture. Because option value is tied to stock price and volatility, you also need to develop a dependable method for evaluation of the underlying stock.

You may pick stocks strictly on the basis of fundamental analysis. This includes a study of financial statements, dividends paid to stockholders, management, the company's position within its industry, capitalization, product or service, and other financial information.

The importance of the fundamentals cannot be emphasized too much, as they define a company's long-term growth prospects, ability to produce consistent profits, and ability to demonstrate market strength over time. However, remember that the fundamentals are historical and have little to do with short-term price changes in the company's stock. It is that very thing—short-term price change—that determines whether a particular option strategy will succeed or fail. While the fundamentals are essential for long-term stock selection, short-term price movement is affected more by perception of value. Indicators involving market price and perception are broadly classified under the umbrella of *technical analysis.*

Both fundamental and technical indicators have something to offer, and you can use elements of both to study and identify stocks for option trading. The distinctions should be kept in mind, however, including both the advantages and disadvantages of each method.

The selection of options cannot be made without also reviewing the attributes of the stock, both fundamental and technical. Whether you treat options only as a form of speculative side bet or as an important aspect associated with being in the market, the judgment you use in selection has to apply to the characteristics and values of both the option and the stock. Criteria for the selection of high-value stocks are at the heart of smart stock market investing. The need for careful, thorough, and continuing analysis cannot be emphasized too much. So attributes such as financial strength, price stability and volatility, dividend and profit history, and others are important, not only to stockholders but to options traders as well. Picking worthwhile options trades depends on your awareness of fundamental and technical indicators for the stock, even while you recognize that short-term indicators may not be reliable.

Key Point

In the stock market, the perception of value is of far greater interest in stock valuation than is the actual fundamental value. Perception in the market carries far more weight than even fact itself.

The analysis of stock values for the purpose of determining whether to buy stock is a complex science. When options are added to the equation, it becomes even more complicated. As shown in Table 1.1, you would consider stock price movement to be either a plus or a minus depending on whether you are planning to operate as a seller or buyer, and whether you plan to utilize calls or puts.

Example

All Around the Money: Two months ago, you bought a call and paid a premium of $300. The striking price was 40 per share. At that time, the underlying stock's price was at $40 per share. In this condition—when the call's striking price is identical to the current market value of the stock—the call is said to be *at the money*. If the market value per share of stock increases so that the per-share value is above the call's striking price, then the call is said to be *in the money*. When the price of the stock decreases so that the per-share value is below the call's striking price, then the call is said to be *out of the money*.

Table 1.1 Price Movement in the Underlying Security

	Increase in Price	Decrease in Price
Call buyer	Positive	Negative
Call seller	Negative	Positive
Put buyer	Negative	Positive
Put seller	Positive	Negative

These definitions are reversed for puts; "in" and "out of" the money occur in the opposite directions. Figure 1.3 shows the price ranges that represent in the money, at the money, and out of the money for a call.

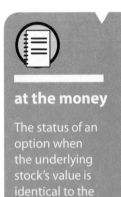

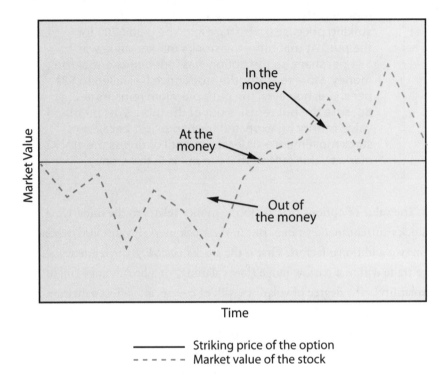

Striking price of the option
Market value of the stock

Figure 1.3 Market Value of the Underlying Stock in Relation to Striking Price of a Call

The dollar-for-dollar price movement of an option's value occurs whenever an option is in the money. The tendency will be for the option's value to mirror price movement in the stock, going up or down to the same degree as the stock's market price. These price movements will not always be identical because, as expiration nears, the time factor also affects the option's value.

In the preceding example, a significant change would occur if the stock's market price continued to fall below the striking price. Once in the money, the put's value would rise one dollar for each dollar of decline in the stock's market value (not considering the time factor).

out of the money

The status of a call option when the underlying stock's market value is lower than the option's striking price, or of a put option when the underlying stock's market value is higher than the option's striking price.

Example

Staying Out of the Money: You bought a put last month with a striking price of 30 and you paid 2. (The striking price is 30 per share and you paid $200 for the put.) At that time, the stock's market value was $34 per share, so the option was four points out of the money. More recently, the stock price has fallen to $31 per share; however, the put's premium remains at 2. Because the put remains out of the money, its premium value cannot be expected to change just because of stock movement—at least not until or unless the stock's market value falls so that the put is in the money.

The value of options that are in the money relates to the underlying stock's current market value. But in the stock market, value also depends on two additional factors. First is the stock's *volatility*, the tendency to trade within a narrow range (low volatility) or a broad range (high volatility). The degree of volatility will, of course, also affect valuation of the option, as will the time element. But value is also affected by *volume*—the level of trading activity in the stock *and* in the option, or in the market as a whole. The level of volume in a stock might have a similar effect on option value, or option volume could be affected by entirely different factors. Options traders look for clues to explain circumstances when option volume increases but no corresponding increase is seen in the stock. That could indicate that other factors, not yet widely recognized in the market, are distorting the option's value or the stock's value, or that other factors (such as unfounded rumors) are causing distortions in both the stock and the option.

volatility

An indicator of the degree of change in a stock's market value, measured over a 12-month period and stated as a percentage. To measure volatility, subtract the lowest 12-month price from the highest 12-month price, and divide the answer by the 12-month lowest price.

Pick the Right Stock

The usual assumption in using any form of analysis is that you identify stocks you would want to buy or hold, and when the news turns bad, you then want to sell shares. With options, however, a stock that shows inherent weaknesses can also signal the time to use options in a different way. For example, if you are convinced that a stock is overpriced and susceptible to price decline, one reaction would be to buy puts. If you're right and the price falls, your puts will increase in value. Thus, the difference between stock investors and options traders is the reaction to news. Stock investors tend to view bad news—price weakness, negative economic news, overpricing of shares, corporate scandals, and so on—as just bad news. An options trader, though, can use any form of news to make a profitable move in options, even when the news is negative for the company and its stockholders.

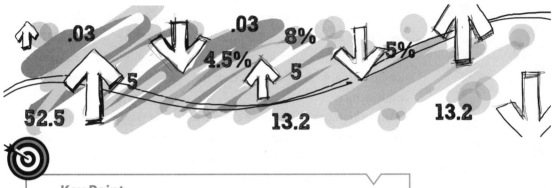

Key Point

Selecting options wisely depends on also identifying or picking stocks using logical criteria. Using options without also analyzing stocks is a big mistake.

Chapter 8 provides a more in-depth study of stock selection criteria. For now, be aware that checking the facts by reviewing corporate information is a smart starting point. A lot of information can be obtained free to let you begin reviewing a corporation's financial strength. You can get current information about any listed company from a number of sources on the Internet. These include several free services allowing downloads of corporate annual reports in addition to direct contact with the companies themselves.

Valuable Resource

Check websites for online subscription services at **www.valueline.com** and **www.standardandpoors.com**

Intrinsic Value and Time Value

Once you become comfortable with methods of stock selection, you will be ready to use that knowledge to study the options market. Remember that options themselves change in value based on movement in the underlying stock. Because option valuation is inescapably tied to stock

intrinsic value

That portion of an option's current value equal to the number of points that it is in the money. One points equals one dollar of value per share, so 35 points equals $35 per share.

value and market conditions, options do not possess any fundamental value of their own. By definition, the fundamentals are the financial condition and results of the corporation; an option is related to the stock's market value and exists only for a brief period of time. Every listed option and its pricing structure are more easily comprehended by a study of valuation, which has two parts.

The first of the two segments of value is called *intrinsic value*, which is that part of an option's premium equal to the number of points it is in the money. Intrinsic value, for example, is three points for a call that is three points above striking price, or for a put that is three points below striking price.

Any option premium above the intrinsic value is known as time value. This will decline predictably over time, as expiration nears. With many months before expiration, time value can be substantial; if the option is at the money or out of the money, the entire premium is time value. As expiration approaches, time value evaporates at a quickening pace, and at the point of expiration, no time value remains. Time value also tends to fall away when the option is substantially out of the money. In other words, an option that is 2 points out of the money will be likely to have greater time value than one with the same time until expiration, but 15 points out of the money.

Option valuation can be summed up in this statement: The relative degree of intrinsic value and time value is determined by the distance between striking price and the current market value of stock, adjusted by the time remaining until expiration of the option.

Example

Value, but No Real Value: A 45 call is valued currently at 3 ($300 premium value on a 45 striking price). The underlying stock's market value is currently $45 per share. Because the option is at the money, it has no intrinsic value. The entire premium represents time value alone. You know that by expiration, the time value will disappear completely, so it will be necessary for the stock to increase in value at least three points for you to break even were you to buy the call (and without considering transaction fees). The stock will need to rise beyond the 3-point level before expiration if you are to earn a profit.

A comparison between option premium and market value of the underlying stock is presented in Table 1.2. Using a call as an example, this table demonstrates the direct relationship between intrinsic value, market value of the underlying stock, and time value of the option. If the option were a put, intrinsic value would be represented by the degree to which the stock's market value was below striking price.

Table 1.2 The Declining Time Value of an Option

Month	Stock Price ($)	Option Premium (Striking Price of 45)		
		Total Value ($)	Intrinsic Value ($)[1]	Time Value ($)[2]
1	45	3	0	3
2	47	5	2	3
3	46	4	1	3
4	46	3	1	2

Month	Stock Price ($)	Option Premium (Striking Price of 45)		
		Total Value ($)	Intrinsic Value ($)[1]	Time Value ($)[2]
5	47	4	2	2
6	44	2	0	2
7	46	2	1	1
8	45	1	0	1
9	46	1	1	0

[1] *Intrinsic value reflects the price difference between the stock's current market value and the option's striking price.*
[2] *Time value is greatest when the expiration date is furthest away and declines as expiration approaches.*

Another helpful illustration is shown in Figure 1.4. This summarizes movement in the underlying stock (top graph) and option values (bottom graph). Note that intrinsic value (dark blue portion) is identical to stock price movement in the money, and that time value moves independently, gradually dissolving as expiration approaches. From this illustration, you can see how the two forms of value act independently from one another, because different influences—stock price versus time—affect the two segments of the option premium.

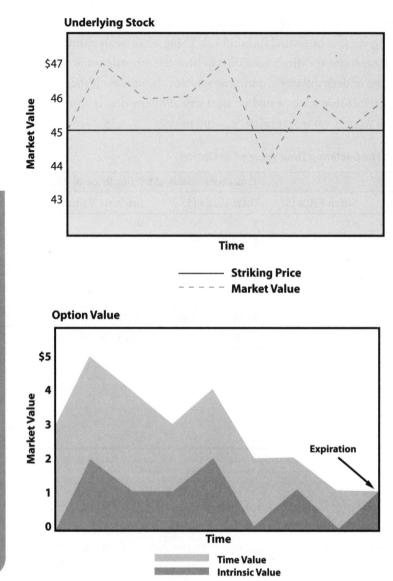

extrinsic value

The portion of an option's premium generated from volatility in the underlying stock and from market perception of potential price changes until expiration date; a nonintrinsic portion of the premium value not specifically caused by the element of time.

Figure 1.4 Time and Intrinsic Values of Underlying Stock and Options

The total amount of option premium can be expected to vary greatly between two different stocks at the same price level and identical option features, due to other influences. These include the perception of value, the stock's price history and volatility, stock trading volume, financial status and trends, interest in options among buyers and sellers, and dozens of other possible influences. For example, two stocks at the same current price may have options at 35 and identical expiration dates. But even given identical features, the option premium could be different for each.

Differences in option value are caused solely by changes in nonintrinsic value. The intrinsic value is always equal to the number of points an option is in the money, and any additional premium is generally classified as time value. (This distinction is a bit more complex, due to the additional value-based elements explained later.)

The non-intrinsic value of an option premium is where all the differences exist. Because intrinsic value is entirely predictable and tied to the difference between stock price and option striking price, it is not difficult to predict at all. Beyond intrinsic value, premium will vary because of the stock's volatility, market perceptions of market risk, and any other market factors that make future price changes uncertain. The uncertainty factor, more than anything else, is the feature of option value that is the most appealing. So the so-called time value premium is where analysis and study will be focused.

In fact, time value is not solely affected by time. It also changes due to the degree of price movement in the stock and, more specifically, is based on perceptions about stock price movement. Time value also varies to some degree due to outside influences, like the market sector of the stock. For example, information technology stocks might be more volatile as a group than pharmaceutical or retail stocks; as a result, time value might also be more volatile for options on those stocks.

Because time value is not defined entirely by time, it can be further broken down into two primary parts. Time value—the portion affected strictly by time—is generally quite predictable. As time until expiration approaches, time value declines on an accelerated basis. And the farther out of the money the option is, the more rapid the decline in time value. But actual volatility in the stock also determines the nonintrinsic option value, and this portion is distinguished from pure time value and is called *extrinsic value*.

So time value itself becomes quite unpredictable and inconsistent due to extrinsic value. If an option is out of the money, there is no intrinsic value involved; but when an option is in the money, premium contains three parts:

1. Intrinsic value is equal to the number of points between current striking price and current stock price.
2. Time value refers to all non-intrinsic value in most discussions. However, in a strict sense, time value is that portion of premium affected by the passage of time and the time remaining until expiration.

3. Extrinsic value is the premium value within time value caused by nontime sources. These include perceived potential for price changes, volatility in the stock, and other external causes.

Throughout the rest of this book, the use of the term time value refers to the entire non-intrinsic premium and includes both time and extrinsic value. The term can be confusing because in some options writings, extrinsic value is used as a substitute for time value. For example, Investopedia defines extrinsic value as "the difference between an option's price and the intrinsic value." While this is not entirely accurate, it does agree with a popular definition but makes no distinction between the attributes of time and nontime segments.

Valuable Resource

To find definitions for thousands of investment terms, check **www.investopedia.com.**

Option buyers, as a rule, will be willing to pay more for options when they perceive a greater than normal potential for price movement. Higher levels of volatility increase risks all around, but also increase potential for bigger profits in option speculation. Of course, low-volatility stocks are going to be far less interesting to would-be option buyers, because little price change is expected in the stock. The same arguments apply to sellers; higher-volatility stocks are accompanied by options with higher time value and more potential for profits from selling options (as well as greater risks for exercise).

You can recognize time value easily by comparing the stock's current value to the option's premium. For example, a stock currently priced at $47 per share may have an option valued at 3 and a striking price of 45. To break down the total option premium, subtract striking price from the current market value; the difference is intrinsic value. Then subtract intrinsic value from total premium to find time value. If premium value is at or below striking price (for a call) or above striking price (for a put), there is no intrinsic value. The preceding example is summarized as follows:

Stock Price	
Current market value of the stock	$47
Less striking price of the option	−45
Intrinsic value	$ 2
Option Premium	
Total premium	$ 3
Less intrinsic value	−2
Time value	$ 1

In the next chapter, several important features of options—striking price, expiration date, and exercise—are more fully explored, especially in light of how these features affect your personal options strategy.

Thomsett's Journey in OPTIONS
EXCUSE ME, BUT I'M CONFUSED BY THE DIFFERENCES BETWEEN CALLS AND PUTS. CAN YOU EXPLAIN?
I COULD, BUT IT MIGHT BE BETTER TO SHOW YOU.

2 OPENING & TRACKING: HOW IT ALL WORKS

Every thinker puts some new portion of an apparently stable world in peril.
—Thomas Dewey, *Characters and Events*, 1929

Every option is characterized by four specific attributes, collectively called the *terms* of the option (also called *standardized terms*). These are striking price, expiration date, type of option (call or put), and the underlying stock.

These are the four essential pieces you need to see the whole picture, to know which option is being discussed, and to distinguish it from all other options. In evaluating risk and potential gain, and even to discuss an option, every buyer and every seller needs to have these four essential pieces of information in hand. Of course, because point of view between buyer and seller will be opposite, an advantageous situation to one person may well be disadvantageous to another. That is the nature of investing in options: You can take a position on one side or the other for any particular option, depending on where you believe the advantage lies.

To review the four terms:

1. *Striking price.* The striking price is the fixed price at which the option can be exercised. It is the pivotal piece of information that determines the relative value of options based on the proximity of a stock's market value; it is the price per share to be paid or received in the event of exercise. The striking price is divisible by 5 points for stocks traded between $30 and $200. When shares trade below $30 per share, options are sold in increments divisible by 2.5 and other issues end up with fractional values after a stock split. Stocks selling above $200 per share have options selling at intervals divisible by 10 points. The striking price remains unchanged during the life of the option, no matter how much change occurs in the market value of the underlying stock. (When stocks split, both striking price and the number of shares have to be adjusted. For example, after a 2-for-1 split, a $45 option would be replaced with two options of $22.50, and the original 100 shares would be replaced with 200 shares of half the value.)

   For the buyer, striking price identifies the price at which 100 shares of stock can be bought (with a call) or sold (with a put). For a seller, striking price is the opposite: It is the price at which 100 shares of stock will be sold (with a call) or bought (with a put) in the event that the buyer decides to exercise.

2. *Expiration date.* Every option exists for only a limited number of months. That can be either a problem or an opportunity, depending upon whether you are acting as a buyer or as a seller, and upon the specific strategies you employ. The LEAPS provides more time, thus more flexibility on the time limitation. It also commands a higher premium as a result. Every option has three possible outcomes. It will eventually be canceled through a closing transaction, be exercised, or expire, but it never goes on forever. Because the option is not tangible, the potential number of active options is unlimited except by market demand. A company issues only so many shares of stock, so buyers and sellers need to adjust prices according to supply and demand. This is not true of options, which have no specific limitations such as numbers issued.

Example

Call for a Strike: You purchase a call with a strike price of 25, which entitles you to buy 100 shares of stock at $25 per share, no matter how high the market price of the stock rises before expiration date. However, the company announces a 2-for-1 stock split. After the split, you own two calls with a strike price of 12.50.

Options active at any given time are limited by the risks involved. An option far out of the money will naturally draw little interest, and those with impending expiration will similarly lose market interest as their time value evaporates. Buyers need to believe there is enough time for a profit to materialize, and that the market price is close enough to the striking price that a profit is realistic; or, if in the money, that it is not so expensive that risks are too great. The same considerations that create disadvantages for buyers represent opportunities for sellers. Pending expiration reduces the likelihood of out-of-the-money options being exercised, and distance between market price of the stock and striking price of the call means the seller's profits are more likely to materialize than are the hopes of the buyer.

Example

Expiring Interest: You bought a put two months ago at striking price of 50. This put expires next week, but today the stock's market value is $55 per share. The put is five points out of the money and its current value is fractional. Unless the stock's market value falls within the next week, this put will expire worthless.

3. *Type of option.* Understanding the distinction between calls and puts is essential to success in the options market; the two are opposites. Identical strategies cannot be used for calls and puts, for reasons beyond the obvious fact that they react to stock price movement differently. Calls are by definition the right to buy 100 shares, whereas puts are the right to sell 100 shares. But merely comprehending the essential opposite nature of the two contracts is not enough.

It might seem at first glance that, given the behavior of calls and puts when in the money or out of the money, it would make no difference whether you buy a put or sell a call. As long as expiration and striking price are identical, what is the difference? In practice, however, significant differences do make these two ideas vastly different in terms of risk. When you buy a put, your risk is limited to the amount you pay for premium. When you sell a call, your risk can be far greater because the stock may rise many points, requiring the call seller to deliver 100 shares at a price far below current market value. Each specific strategy has to be reviewed in terms not only of likely price movement given a set of market price changes in the underlying stock, but also how one's position is affected by exposure to varying degrees of risk.

Example

Put Me Down for a Call: You have bought two options on two different stocks. The first one, a call, has a striking price of 25. When you bought it, the stock was at $23 per share, but today it has risen to $28. You can sell the call at a profit or exercise it and buy 100 shares at $25 per share. The second option is a put with a strike price of 45. When you bought it, the stock was at $47 per share and you believed the market value would fall. Now, close to expiration, the stock is still at $47 per share and your put has declined in value. The call value increases when stock value rises; and the put value increases when stock value falls.

4. *Underlying stock.* Every option is identified with a specific company's stock, and this cannot be changed. Listed options are not offered on all stocks traded, nor are they available on every stock exchange. (Some options trade on only one exchange, while others trade on several.) Options can exist only when a specific underlying stock has been identified, since it is the stock's market value that determines the option's related premium value. All options traded on a specific underlying stock are referred to as a single *class* of options. Thus, a single stock might be associated with a wide variety of calls and puts with different striking prices and expiration months, but they all belong to the same class. In comparison, all those options with the same combination of terms—identical striking prices, expiration date, type (call or put), and underlying stock—are considered a single *series* of options.

Example

Stuck with the Stock: You bought calls a couple of months ago in a pharmaceutical stock, in the belief that it would rise in value. You realize now that you picked the wrong company. The one on which you hold calls has been lackluster, but a competitor's stock has risen dramatically. You would like to transfer your calls over to the other company, but the rules won't allow you to do this. Every option is identified strictly with one company and cannot be transferred.

A NOTE ON THE EXPIRATION CYCLE

Expiration dates for options of a single underlying stock are offered on a predictable *cycle*. Every stock with listed options can be identified by the cycle to which it belongs, and these remain unchanged. There are three annual cycles:

1. January, April, July, and October (JAJO)
2. February, May, August, and November (FMAN)
3. March, June, September, and December (MJSD)

In addition to these fixed expiration cycle dates, active options are available for expiration in the upcoming month. For example, let's suppose that a particular stock has options expiring in the cycle month of April. In February, you may be able to trade in short-term options expiring in March (even though that is not a part of the normal cyclical expiration). Some underlying securities also have weekly options, creating two expirations in the nearest month.

Expiration cycles for LEAPS options are quite different. All LEAPS contracts expire in January. At any given time, you can find an open LEAPS option for the next two January expiration dates and by midyear a third one is also available. This means that you can keep a LEAPS contract open as long as 30 months (up to 2 years) based on these cycles.

> **Key Point**
>
> Some options traders use short-term options as speculative devices. Because they come and go more rapidly than the cyclical options, they often are overlooked as opportunities. For example, they can be used to temporarily protect longer-term short option positions.

An option's expiration takes place on the third Saturday of the expiration month. An order to close an open position has to be placed and executed no later than the *last trading day* before expiration day, and before the indicated *expiration time* for the option. As a general rule, this means that the trade has to be executed before the close of business on the Friday immediately before the Saturday of expiration; however, a specific cutoff time could be missed on an exceptionally busy Friday, so you need to ensure that your broker is going to be able to execute your trade in time to comply with the rules.

The last-minute order that you place can be one of three types of transactions. It can be an order to buy in order to close a currently open (previously sold) short position; an order to sell an existing long position to close; or an exercise order to buy or to sell 100 shares of stock for each option involved. If a last-minute exercise is made against your short position, the order is entered without your advance knowledge; you are advised of exercise and instructed to deliver funds (for an exercised call) or to accept and pay for shares (for an exercised put).

expiration time

The latest possible time to place an order for cancellation or exercise of an option, which may vary depending on the brokerage firm executing the order and on the option itself.

Example

A Matter of Timing: You bought a call scheduled to expire in the month of July. Its expiration occurs on the third Saturday in that month. You need to place a sell order or an order to exercise the call (to buy 100 shares of stock at the striking price) before expiration time on the preceding Friday, which is the last trading day prior to expiration. If you fail to place either a sell or exercise order by that time, the option will expire worthless and you will receive no benefit. With the pending deadline in mind and the unknown potential for a busy Friday in the market—which can occur whether you place orders over the telephone or on the Internet—you need to place that order with adequate time for execution. You can place the order far in advance with instructions to execute it by the end of business on Friday. If the brokerage firm accepts that order, then you will be protected if they fail to execute—as long as you placed the order well in advance of the deadline.

Key Point

Even though expiration time is the end of the trading day, it makes practical sense to place a last-day order well before that time—and to place the order without restrictions. Only a market order will get executed, so specifying a desired price could prevent the order from going through.

OPENING AND CLOSING OPTION TRADES

Every option trade you make must specify the four terms: striking price, expiration month, call or put, and the underlying stock. If any of these terms changes, that means that an entirely different option is involved.

Whenever you have opened an option by buying or selling, the status is called an *open position*. As soon as the open position is offset by a closing transaction, it becomes a *closed position*. When you buy, it is described as an *opening purchase transaction*. And if you start out by selling an option, that is called an *opening sale transaction*.

Example

Open and Close: You bought a call two months ago. When you entered your order, it was an opening purchase transaction. That status remains the same as long as you take no further action. The position will be closed when you enter a *closing sale transaction to* sell the call. You may also exercise the option; if you do not take either of these actions, the option will expire.

OPEN POSITION

OPENING PURCHASE/SALE TRANSACTION

Using the Daily Options Listings

Online trading is a natural for the options market. The ability to monitor a changing market on the basis of only a 20-minute delay is a significant advantage over telephone calls to a broker, and for an extra charge you can get real-time quotations (or as close as possible to real time) online. The Internet is also likely to be far more responsive than a broker, who may be on another line, with another client, or away from the desk when you call. For you as an options trader, even a few minutes of inaccessibility can create a lost opportunity. Of course, exceptionally heavy volume market periods translate to slowdowns, even on the Internet.

In the past, options traders depended on alert brokers, hoping the brokers would be able to telephone them if price changes made fast decisions necessary. Some placed stop limit orders, a cumbersome method for managing an options portfolio. And in the worst of all cases, some investors used to wait until the day after to review options listings in the newspaper. None of these antiquated methods are adequate for the modern options trader, who should be able to find a dependable online source for rapid options quotations.

Valuable Resource

You can make good use of online sites offering free options and stock quotes. Three sites with exceptional quotation services are quote.com **(www.quote.com)**, etrade **(www.etrade.com)**, and Yahoo! Finance **(http://finance.yahoo.com)**. You can also go directly to the Chicago Board Options Exchange (CBOE) to get detailed options quotes **(www.cboe.com)** or check the major exchanges **(www.nyse.com, www.nasdaq.com,** and **www.amex.com)**.

Not only are you more able to work on your own through discount service brokers and without expensive and unneeded broker advice; you also need to be online to maximize your market advantage. Option pricing can change from minute to minute in many situations, and you need to be able to keep an eye on the market.

Whether you use an automated system or published options service, you also need to learn how to read options listings. A typical daily options listing from the month of March 2012 is summarized in Table 2.1.

Table 2.1 Example of Daily Options Listing

Walmart (WMT)	Striking Price	Calls			Puts		
		Apr	May	Jun	Apr	May	Jun
60.72	60	1.23	1.63	1.88	0.55	1.15	1.40
60.72	62.50	0.18	0.47	0.66	2.11	2.60	2.80
60.72	65	0.02	0.10	0.19	4.30	5.05	5.05
60.72	67.50	0.01	0.00	0.04	6.50	9.85	9.10

The details of what this table shows are:

First column: The underlying stock and the current market value of the stock. In this example, Walmart's current price was $60.72 per share.

Second column: This shows the striking price for each available option. The example includes options with striking prices between 60 and 67.50 per share. In this particular case, Walmart included options in between the normal five-point increments.

Third, fourth, and fifth columns: These show current premium levels for calls. Note two trends. As striking prices rise farther above current market value, call values decline; and as time until expiration extends outward, call values rise.

Sixth, seventh, and eighth columns: These show current premium levels for puts. The same two trends are evident here. However, because put valuation moves in a direction opposite that of calls, the farther in the money, the higher the put value. For example, the $67.50 put is almost 7 points in the money. This is reflected in the higher premium value, and additional time further adds to put valuation.

In this example, Walmart trades on the March, June, September, December (MJSD) cycle. However, in all cases, the three months following the current month always have options as well. The report was taken in March, so options are available for March, April, and May (and then for June, September, and December).

For LEAPS, the same information is available but for longer terms. For comparable LEAPS listings, see Table 2.2.

Table 2.2 Example of LEAPS Listings

Walmart (WMT)	Striking Price	Calls Jan 13	Calls Jan 14	Puts Jan 13	Puts Jan 14
60.72	60	3.40	5.40	3.65	6.70
60.72	62.50	2.18	—	4.90	—
60.72	65	1.28	3.45	6.50	10.80
60.72	67.50	0.72	—	10.75	—

In this example, premium values are considerably higher for the same range of striking prices. Since there is much more time until expiration, time value is also higher for the LEAPS options. This opens up a broader range of strategic possibilities for both buyers and sellers. LEAPS contracts always expire in January each year, so as of March, 2012, the long-term values show January expirations only. Also, the interim values for LEAPS ($62.50 and $67.50) were not available for Walmart two years out; thus, no current value exists for those valuations.

Understanding Option Abbreviations

In 2010, the Options Clearing Corporation (OCC) did away with the outdated system of option symbols and replaced it. The old system was outdated because it did not provide for options whose expiration was more than one year out. This led to great confusion in the market.

Today, the options symbol is longer than before but much easier to understand. Every listed option now reports the entire date of expiration, including the four-digit year. For example, Figure 2.1 shows an example of a complete options listing.

Figure 2.1 The Complete Options Listing

This is an options listing for McDonalds (MCD) expiring in the month of November (11), on the 19th, and in the year 2011. The striking price is also shown (92.50) and this is a call (C).

The method of expressing options used among traders and brokers also takes getting used to. This occurs in abbreviated form. For example, given the McDonald's listing, a trader will refer to this as an "MCD November 92.50 call."

In writing down values for options and related stocks, the following style guidelines apply:

- When referring to stock market values, always use dollar signs and dollars and cents: $91.78, not 91.78.
- The striking price of an option is always given in dollars and cents, but without dollar signs: 92.50, not $92.50.
- The options quote is always given as value per share to two decimal places, and without dollar signs. So when you see 4.63 it means that option's current premium is $463.
- The month is abbreviated in text but not expressed numerically. Thus, the November expiration in this case is "Nov. 92.50" and not the "11 92.50."
- Expiration day is rarely expressed other than in the listing itself. Traders know that the last trading day is the third Friday of expiration month and expiration date is the third Saturday.
- Exception: When two active options expire in the same month but on different days, the specific expiration day must be included. This happens when current-month weekly options are active, for example. You may have expirations for the weekly as well as the monthly cycle.

The method of expressing options premium values and underlying stock values is intended to make the markets work efficiently. Given the complexity of jargon and the various numerical values expressed by traders and brokers, these sensible rules help avoid misunderstandings.

Valuable Resource

For free LEAPS listings and a wide range of other LEAPS resources, check the CBOE website "quotes" link at **www.cboe.com/delayedquote.**

CALCULATING THE RATE OF RETURN FOR SELLERS

You are guided by your *rate of return* in all your investments. In a single transaction involving one buy and one sell, rate of return is easily calculated. Simply divide the net profit (after trading fees) by the total purchase amount (including trading fees), and the resulting percentage is the rate of return. When you sell options, though, the rate of return is more complicated. The sale precedes the purchase, so rate of return is not as straightforward as it is in the more traditional investment.

Rate of return can only be looked at in comparative form. In other words, comparing one short position outcome to another, given dissimilar holding periods, makes the comparison invalid. The calculation should be adjusted so that all short position outcomes are reviewed and compared on an *annualized basis*. Because different lengths of time can be involved in a short position—from a few hours up to several months, or even two to three years if LEAPS are involved—it is not realistic to compare calculated rates of return without making the adjustment. A 50 percent return in two months is far more significant than the same rate of return with a 10-month holding period.

rate of return

The yield from investing, calculated by dividing net cash profit upon sale by the amount spent at purchase.

Example

When 12 Percent Is Not 12 Percent: You realize a net profit of 12 percent on an investment. The annualized rate of return will vary depending on the holding period.

1. Three months:
    Net profit 12%
    Holding period = 3 months
    12 ÷ 3 = 4%
    4% × 12 months = 48% annualized

2. Eight months:
    Net profit 12%
    Holding period = 8 months
    12 ÷ 8 = 1.5%
    1.5% × 12 months = 18% annualized

3. Fifteen months:
    Net profit 12%
    Holding period = 15 months
    12 ÷ 15 = 0.8%

annualized basis

A method for comparing rates of return for holdings of varying periods, in which all returns are expressed as though investments had been held over a full year. It involves dividing the rate of return by the number of months the positions were open, and multiplying the result by 12.

0.8% × 12 months = 9.6% annualized

To annualize a rate of return, follow these three steps:

1. Calculate the rate of return. Divide the net profit by the amount of purchase.
2. Divide the rate of return by the number of months the investment position was open.
3. Multiply the result by 12 (months).

As these examples demonstrate, annualized rate of return differs dramatically depending on the period the position remained open. Annualizing applies for periods above one year, as in example number 3. A short period is properly extended though annualizing, just as a period beyond one year should be contracted to reflect rate of return as *though* the investment were held for exactly 12 months. By making all returns comparable, it becomes possible to study the outcomes realistically, not to calculate your true average yield but to better be able to analyze outcomes side by side. Annualizing can also produce exceptional but unrealistic results. So, annualizing is valuable for making accurate comparisons, but it will not necessarily provide you with a realistic future average return using options. You should accept the possibility that you will experience a range of outcomes from options trading; some profits materialize quickly, and others take a long time. Some strategies will also produce losses. The calculation of return is made even more complex when it involves more than return on the option premium. When you sell calls against stock you own, you need to adjust the comparative analysis to study the likely outcome based on two possible events. The first is called *return if exercised*. This is the rate of return you will earn if your short call is exercised and 100 shares of stock are called away. It includes both the profit on your option and profit or loss on the stock, as well as any dividends you received during the period you owned the stock.

Example

Fast Turnaround: You recently sold a call at 3 and, only two weeks later, closed the position by buying at 1. The profit, $200, is 4,800 percent on an annualized basis (200 percent return divided by 0.5 month, and multiplied by 12 months, or [200 ÷ 0.5] × 12). This is impressive, but it is of little use in your comparative analysis. Not only is it atypical of the returns you earn from options trading, but it also reflects an exceptionally brief holding period, which you probably cannot duplicate consistently.

Key Point

Annualized basis is helpful in judging the success of a series of transactions employing a particular strategy. It is less useful in looking at individual outcomes, especially those with very short holding periods.

The second calculation is called *return if unchanged*. This is a calculation of the return to be realized if the stock is not called away and the option is allowed to expire worthless (or it is closed out through a *closing purchase transaction*).

In both types of return, the calculations take into account all forms of income. The major difference between the two rates has to do with profit or loss on the underlying stock. These factors complicate the previous observation that comparisons should be made on an annualized rate. It is extremely difficult to account for each dividend payment, especially if the stock has been held over many years. In addition, how do you account for the return on stock held but not sold?

Neither of these analytical tools lends itself to annualized return, which is a valuable tool for the study of relatively simple transactions involving only one source of income. The return if exercised and return if unchanged are far more valuable as a method for determining the wisdom of a decision to sell a call *in advance* of actually taking that step. By comparing these potential rates of return, you can determine which options are more likely to yield profits adequate to justify tying up 100 shares of stock with a short call position.

The actual steps involved in calculation should always be net of brokerage fees, both for sale and purchase. Remember that no attempt should be made to make comparisons on an annualized basis, however, because complex transactions with differing types of profit, and generated over different lengths of time, make annualized return inappropriate. While the following examples use single-option contracts, in practice options traders often use multiple options and involve more than 100 shares of stock.

Example

Many Happy Returns: You own 100 shares of stock that you purchased originally at $58 per share. Current market value is $63 per share. You sell a call with a striking price of 60 and receive a premium of 7. Between the date the option is sold and expiration, you also receive two dividend payments, totaling $68.

Return if exercised:	
Striking price	6,000
Less original cost of stock	−5,800
Profit on stock	$200
Dividends received	68
Call premium received	+700
Total profit	$968
Return if exercised: ($968 ÷ $5,800) = 16.69%	

Return if unchanged:	
Call premium received	$700
Dividends received	$68
Total profit	$768
Return if unchanged: ($768 ÷ $5,800) = 13.24%	

This side-by-side calculation allows you to see what will happen in either outcome. In the example, it comes down to a difference of about 3.5 percent between the two outcomes. So the question becomes, would it be worth that small difference to accept exercise? In the alternative, would it be better to close out the position before expiration and repeat the transaction subsequently? By avoiding exercise, you can sell a later call and expand profits even further, which should also be considered when comparing these two possible outcomes.

The comparison between "if exercised" and "if unchanged" is further complicated by inclusion of capital gain on the stock. Because one calculation includes this and the other does not, the two outcomes are not truly comparable. Based on the striking price you pick when you sell a call against 100 shares of stock you own, a capital gain could be minimal or quite significant; exercise could even end up with a capital loss, so the gain on the stock cannot be entirely ignored.

Even so, the comparison including stock does distort any attempt to make a true comparison. Ideally, you should consider the corresponding gain or loss on the option only, and separate out capital gains or losses on the stock separately. This is inaccurate, of course, but making valid comparisons of potential outcomes is difficult. The last chapter in this book examines return calculations in more detail, because the difficulty involved makes it especially complex.

Another important factor in this example involves taxes. Because the example includes selling an in-the-money call, the capital gain may be treated as short-term. As part of your option strategy, any short positions have to be made with a tax calculation in mind. A net profit comparison should always include brokerage fees and both federal and state tax consequences, which are going to vary by individual as well as by state.

Annualizing the returns if exercised or if unchanged is not recommended because the transactions involve three different time periods: for stock, dividend, and short position in the call. In addition, the purpose here is not to compare results after the transaction has been completed, but to make a comparison in advance to determine whether the transaction would be worthwhile. You can use these calculations not only to compare the two outcomes, but also to compare outcomes between two or more possible option short positions.

Key Point

The purpose in comparing returns on option selling is not to decide which outcome is more desirable, but to decide whether to enter into the transaction in the first place.

Succeeding in options trading means entering open positions with complete awareness of all possible outcomes and their consequences or benefits. You need to know when it makes sense to close out a position with a closing transaction, avoid exercise with subsequent trades, or just wait for expiration. You also need to be aware of market conditions and the timing of options trades, as well as the relative degree of risk to which you are exposed by entering into open options positions. Knowledge about potential profit is only part of a more complex picture. The more you study options and participate in the market, the more skill you develop in making an overall assessment and comparison.

EVERY OPTION ALSO HAS A FIXED PRICE FOR EXERCISE, CALLED THE STRIKE OR STRIKING PRICE.

CAN THAT BE CHANGED TO A DIFFERENT PRICE?

YOU SAID THERE WERE FOUR, JUST LIKE THE NUMBER OF SLICES ON THIS PIZZA.

HEY, THAT'S THE LAST PIECE. I'M CALLING YOU ON IT. PUT THAT BACK.

NO, LIKE ALL TERMS THE STRIKING PRICE IS FIXED.

3 BUYING CALLS: MAXIMIZING THE ROSY VIEW

More are taken in by hope than by cunning.
—Luc de Clapiers, *Reflections and Maxims*, ca. 1747

Option buyers have to be optimists. They believe a stock's price will move enough points within a limited time to produce a profit. If they are right, their return on investment is huge. If they are wrong, they are 100 percent wrong.

When you embark on a program of buying calls, you take the most speculative position that is possible with options. Since time works against you, substantial change in the underlying stock is required in order to produce a profit. Remember, a call grants to the buyer the right to purchase 100 shares of the underlying stock, at an established striking price per share, and before a firm expiration date in the near-term future. As the buyer, you acquire that right in exchange for paying a premium. You face three alternatives: First, you can sell the call before it expires; second, you can exercise the call and purchase 100 shares of the underlying stock; or third, you can allow the call to expire worthless.

As a call buyer, you are never obligated to buy 100 shares. In comparison, the seller must deliver 100 shares upon exercise of a call. As buyer, you have the right to determine which of the three outcomes will occur. The decision depends on:

- Price movement of the underlying stock and the resulting effect on the call's premium value.
- Your reasons for buying the call in the first place and how related strategies are affected through ownership of the call.
- Your risk posture and willingness to wait for future price movement of both stock and the call, as opposed to taking a profit or cutting a loss today. (This is where setting and following standards comes into play.)

UNDERSTANDING THE LIMITED LIFE OF THE CALL

You can become a call buyer simply for the potential profit you could earn within a limited period of time—in other words, buying purely on the chance of earning a profit in the short term. That profit will be realized if and when the call's premium value increases, so that the call can be sold for more than it cost, or by exercising the call and buying 100 shares of stock below current market value. The call also can be used to offset losses in a short position held in the underlying stock. These uses of calls are explored in more detail later in this chapter.

Valuable Resource

The Options Clearing Corporation publishes a year-long expiration calendar. To see the current version, go to **www. theocc.com/about/publications/expiration-calendar.jsp**.

The buyer's risks are not the same as those for sellers; in fact, they often are the exact opposite. Before becoming an options buyer, examine all the risks, become familiar with potential losses as well as potential gains, and review risk from both sides: as potential buyer or seller. Time value evaporates with ever-increasing speed as expiration nears, which is a disadvantage to you as a buyer but an advantage to the seller. Time is a significant factor that affects your decision about when to close out your

long position in the option. Because time value disappears by the point of expiration, time itself dictates which options you can afford to buy, and which ones are long shots. More time value usually means more time until expiration, and more price movement that you will need to make a profit. In fact, even when the stock price movement goes the way you want, you still might not make a profit; price movement has to exceed the number of points of time value and more to produce a profit.

This is where comparisons between listed options and LEAPS options become interesting. For example, you might look at side-by-side options with identical striking prices and come to different conclusions about their viability.

 Example

Into the Stretch: A stock is currently valued at $48 per share. The 50 call expires in eight months and is currently selling for 3. If you buy that call, it will be necessary for the stock to rise at least 5 points to $53 per share before expiration, just to cover your costs before trading fees (such a rise would produce intrinsic value of 3 points, producing breakeven before trading fees).

Which of these scenarios is better? You can buy a short-term call for 3 or a long-term LEAPS call for 9. Depending on the stock and its price volatility, your opinion about future price movement, and your personal risk profile, you could decide to go with either of these calls, or decide to take no action.

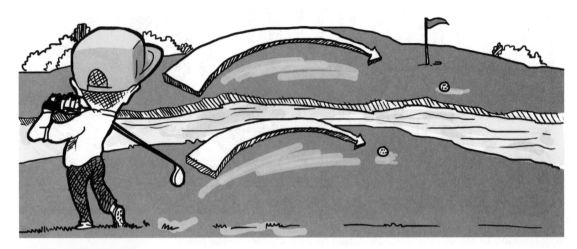

Buying short-term options or LEAPS options are not your only choices. A comparison between purchasing stock as a long-term investment and purchasing calls for short-term profit points out the difference between investment and *speculation*. Typically, speculators accept the risk of loss in exchange for the potential for profit, and they take their positions in short-term instruments such as options for the exposure to that potential. Because a relatively small amount of money can be used to tie up 100 shares of stock, call buying is one form of *leverage*, a popular strategy for making investment capital go further. Of course, the greater the degree of leverage, the greater the associated risk.

speculation

The use of money to assume risks for short-term profit, in the knowledge that substantial or total losses are one possible outcome. Buying calls for leverage is one form of speculation. The buyer may earn a very large profit in a matter of days, or could lose the entire amount invested.

Example

Taking the LEAPS: The picture is far different when a LEAPS call is reviewed. For the same stock, currently valued at $48, the 50 call that expires in 29 months is valued at 9. In this situation, the call costs three times more—$900 versus $300—but you have 30 months for the stock to move, instead of 8 months. You would need the stock to rise 11 points, to $59 per share, to break even in this case.

Key Point

Annualized basis is helpful in judging the success of a series of transactions employing a particular strategy. It is less useful in looking at individual outcomes, especially those with very short holding periods.

When you consider the interaction between intrinsic and time value of calls, you quickly realize that time itself plays a very crucial role in option value. The longer the time until expiration, the more complicated this relationship becomes. For this reason, the LEAPS option presents many interesting possibilities for speculators.

Intrinsic value rises and falls to match the underlying stock's price. But because a LEAPS call is long-term, the action of time value often obscures the relationship between intrinsic value and underlying stock price. It might appear as though the call's value is not tracking the stock point for point. With a lot of time value remaining in a call's premium (including both time and extrinsic segments), it is possible that the call's value will not respond to changes in the stock as clearly as it does when expiration is imminent.

leverage

The use of investment capital in a way that a relatively small amount of money enables the investor to control a relatively large value. This is achieved through borrowing—for example, using borrowed money to purchase stocks or bonds—or through the purchase of options, which exist for only a short period of time but enable the option buyer to control 100 shares of stock. As a general rule, the use of leverage increases potential for profit as well as for loss.

Example

Making the Long Call: You purchased a LEAPS call last month with a striking price two points above market value of the underlying stock. Since then, the stock's price has risen and the LEAPS call is now in the money. But you have noticed that as the stock's market value rises and falls, the LEAPS call tends to duplicate the change only about 75 percent (so when the stock rises one point, the call rises 75 cents). This is caused by changes in perception of extrinsic value, offsetting the tendency of intrinsic value by itself.

The complexity here is that intrinsic value is not entirely isolated from the call's extrinsic value. Two things occur as expiration nears. First, the pure time value premium tends to deteriorate at an accelerated rate. Second, extrinsic value is likely to disappear altogether. If you think of extrinsic value as "potential value" of the call, it makes sense. In other words, extrinsic value exists because of perception that profits may be possible in the call position due to (1) time remaining until expiration; (2) volatility of the underlying stock; and (3) proximity of the striking price and current market value. So in the case of a LEAPS call with many months to go until expiration, a change in the underlying stock will also affect perceptions about the investment or speculative value of the call. Extrinsic value is then likely to affect option value directly.

As expiration approaches, extrinsic value becomes a smaller factor and will disappear from the picture altogether. But as long as many months remain until expiration, intrinsic value cannot operate independently. Some nonintrinsic changes will occur as well. This may be seen as point changes lower than changes in the underlying stock's value, or point changes higher than the point change in the underlying stock. That is the effect of extrinsic value interacting not only with time but also with intrinsic value.

Is call speculation appropriate for you? Questioning risk levels is necessary for every investor and should be an ongoing process of self-examination. Knowing exactly what you are getting into, determining the best strategy, and fully comprehending the risk add up to the measure of your *suitability* for a particular investment or strategy. Suitability identifies what is appropriate given your income, sophistication, experience, understanding of markets and risks, and capital resources. Avoid the problem of understanding the profit potential of a strategy but not the full extent of risk.

Example

My Friend Told Me: An investor has no experience in the market, having never owned stock; he also does not understand how the market works. He has $1,000 available to invest today, and decides that he wants to earn a profit as quickly as possible. A friend told him that big profits can be made buying calls. He wants to buy three calls at 3 each, requiring $900, plus trading fees. He expects to double his money within one month.

This investor would not meet the minimum suitability standards for buying calls. He does not understand the market, know the risks, or appreciate the specific details of options beyond what a friend told him. He probably does not know anything about time value and the chance of losing money from buying calls. He is aware of only the profit potential, and that information is incomplete. In this situation, the broker is responsible for recognizing that option buying would not be appropriate. One of the broker's duties is to ensure that clients know what they are doing and understand all the risks. The broker's duty is to refuse to execute the transaction. This does not mean that every broker will follow that rule.

Suitability refers not only to your ability to afford losses, but also to your understanding of the many forms of risk in the options market. If the investor in the preceding example worked with an experienced broker at the onset, it would also make sense to listen to that broker's advice about a proposed option position.

JUDGING THE CALL

Most call buyers lose money. Even with thorough understanding of the market and trading experience, this fact cannot be overlooked. This statement has to be qualified, however. Most call buyers who simply buy calls for speculation lose money. There are many additional reasons for buying calls, and there are specific strategies to avoid loss.

The biggest problem for call buyers is lack of enough time. Typically, an underlying stock's value rises, but not enough to offset the declining time value by the point of expiration. So if the stock rises, but not enough, then the call buyer will not be able to earn a profit. A simple rise in stock price is not adequate in every case, and call buyers have to recognize the need for not just price change, but *adequate* price change to offset declining time value.

Example

Whem Four Equals Two: You recently bought a call for 4 when it was at $45, at the money (the current market value of the underlying stock was identical to the call's striking price). By expiration, the stock had risen to $47 per share, but the call was worth only 2. Why? The original $400 premium consisted entirely of time value and contained no intrinsic value. The time value was gone by expiration. The $200 value at closing represents the two points of intrinsic value. In this case, you can either sell the call and get half your money back, or wait it out hoping for a last-minute surge in the stock's price. Otherwise, you may simply allow the call to expire and lose the entire $400.

It is a mistake to assume that a call's premium value will rise with the stock in every case, even when in the money. The time value declines as expiration nears, so a rise in the option's premium occurs in intrinsic value, and may only offset lost time value premium. It is likely that even a rising stock price will not reflect dollar-for-dollar gains in the option until the time value has been used up. That's because time value is soft and is likely to evaporate quickly, as opposed to the hard intrinsic value that is more predictable—it changes point for point with in-the-money stock price movement.

Key Point

The increase in premium value of an in-the-money option takes place in intrinsic value. Time value has to be absorbed, too, and as expiration approaches, time value evaporates with increasing speed.

This means that if you buy a call with several points of time value, you cannot earn a profit unless the stock rises enough to (1) offset the time value premium, and (2) create enough growth above striking price. This double requirement is easy to overlook, but worth remembering.

Example

All for Nothing: You bought a call two months ago and paid 1. At the time, the stock was 7 points out of the money. Now the expiration date has arrived. The stock's market value has increased an impressive 6 points. However, the option is virtually worthless because, with expiration pending, there is no intrinsic value. The call is still out of the money, even though the underlying stock's market value has increased 6 points.

Call buyers will lose money if they fail to recognize the requirement that the underlying stock needs to increase sufficiently in value. A mere increase is not enough if time value needs to be offset as well. With this in mind, call buyers should set goals for themselves, defining when to leave a position. The goal should relate to gain and to bailout in the case of a loss.

This is always a problem for anyone taking up a long position with options. You buy hoping the call will grow in value, but time works against you. In fact, three-quarters of all options expire worthless, so making a profit consistently buying options is a difficult task. You need to overcome time as well as realizing growth in intrinsic value; and, of course, interim changes in extrinsic value further complicate this requirement. As a buyer, you race against time. It makes a lot of sense to set goals for yourself, but the time may also come when you realize you are not going to make a profit because time is evaporating. With this in mind, your goal should include identifying when to take a loss.

Key Point

Knowing when to take a profit is only a part of the option trader's goal. It is equally important to know when to take a loss.

Example

Keeping Promises: You are the type of investor who believes in setting goals for yourself. So when you bought a call at 4, you promised yourself you would sell if the premium value fell to 2 or rose to 7. This standard reduces losses in the event that the option declines in value, while also providing a point at which the profit will be taken. You recognize that when it comes to options, time is the enemy and an opportunity might not return. Option buyers often do not get a second chance.

paper profits

Also called *unrealized profits*; values existing only on paper but not taken at the time. Paper profits (or paper losses) become realized only if a closing transaction is executed.

Goal-setting is important because *realized profits* can occur only when you actually close the position. For buyers, that means executing a closing sale transaction. You need to set a standard and then stick to it. Otherwise, you can only watch the potential for realized profits come and go. Your *paper profits* (also known as *unrealized profits*) may easily end up as losses.

If you buy a call and the stock experiences an unexpected jump in market value, it is possible that the time value will increase as well, but this will be temporary; to realize the profit, it has to be taken when it exists. The wider the out-of-the-money range, the lower your chances for realizing a profit. The leverage value of options takes place when the option is in the money. Then the intrinsic value will change point-for-point with the stock. As shown in Figure 3.1, whenever a stock is 5 points or more below the call's striking price, it is described as being *deep out* of the money. For puts, the number of points is the same, but the stock's market value would be 5 points or more above striking price. If the stock's market value is 5 points or more above striking price (for calls) or below striking price (for puts), it is said to be *deep in* the money.

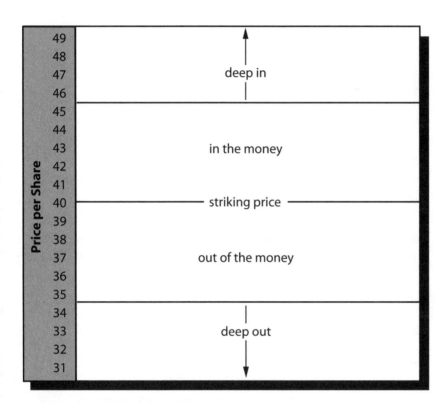

Figure 3.1 Deep In/Deep Out Stock Prices for Calls

deep out

Condition when the underlying stock's current market value is 5 points or more below the striking price of the call or above the striking price of the put.

deep in

Condition when the underlying stock's current market value is 5 points or more above the striking price of the call or below the striking price of the put.

These definitions are important to call buyers. A deep-out-of-the-money option, because it requires significant price movement just to get to a breakeven point, is a long shot; and a deep-in-the-money call is going to demand at least 5 points of premium just for intrinsic value, in addition to its time value. So the majority of call buyers will buy within the 5-point range on either side of the striking price. This provides the maximum opportunity for profit with the least requirement for price increase to offset time value.

CALL BUYING STRATEGIES

Buying calls and hoping they increase in value is a basic, speculative strategy. It is the best-known option strategy, as well. More investors select calls than puts because they tend to think that prices are always going to rise; it is also an obvious strategy. But looking beyond this is where calls become the most interesting. Calls can also be put to work in ways beyond mere speculation.

Strategy 1: Calls for Leverage

Leverage is using a small amount of capital to control a larger investment. While the term usually is applied to borrowing money to invest, it also perfectly describes call buying. For a few hundred dollars placed at risk, you control 100 shares of stock. By "control," I mean that the option buyer has the right (but not the obligation) to buy the 100 shares at any time prior to expiration, with the price frozen by contract. Leverage enables you to establish the potential for profit with a limited amount of at-risk capital. This is why so many call buyers willingly assume the risks, even knowing that the odds of making money on the call itself are against them.

Example

Spotting the Advantage: You are familiar with a pharmaceutical company's management, profit history, and product line. The company has recently announced that it has received approval for the release of a new drug. The release date is three months away. However, the market has not yet responded to the news. You expect that the stock's market price will rise substantially once the market realizes the significance of the new drug. But you are not sure; the lack of response by the market has raised some doubt in your mind. By buying a call with six months until expiration, you expose yourself to a limited risk; but the opportunity for gain is also worth that risk, in your opinion. In this case, you have not risked the price of 100 shares, only the relatively small cost of the option.

Profits can take place rapidly in an option's value. If the price of the stock were to take off, you would have a choice: You could sell the call at a profit, or exercise it and pick up 100 shares at a fixed price below market value. That is a wise use of leverage, given the circumstances described. Things can change quickly. This can be demonstrated by comparing the risks between the purchase of 100 shares of stock, versus the purchase of a call. (See Figure 3.2.)

Example

Expanded Potential: Given the same circumstances as in the previous example, you also realize that price growth might not occur for one to two years. It may require market response and acceptance, so a short-term option will not provide the leverage you seek. A LEAPS call does provide you the long-term leverage in this situation. Buying a LEAPS call will require more investment, because you have to buy the additional time; but if you believe the stock has growth potential within the window of time, it would make sense to invest.

	Stock[1]		Call[2]	
	Profit or Loss	Rate of Return	Profit or Loss	Rate of Return
Price increase of 5 points	$500	8.1%	$500	100%
Price increase of 1 point	$100	1.6%	$100	20%
No price change	0	0	0	0
Price decrease of 1 point	–$100	–1.6%	–$100	–20%
Price decrease of 5 points	–$500	–8.1%	–$500	–100%
[1] Purchased at $62 per share ($6,200). [2] Striking price 60, premium 5 ($500).				

Figure 3.2 Rate of Return: Buying Stocks versus Calls

settlement date

The date on which a buyer is required to pay for purchases, or on which a seller is entitled to receive payment. For stocks, settlement date is three business days after the transaction. For options, settlement date is one business day from the date of the transaction.

In this example, the stock was selling at $62 per share. You could invest $6,200 and buy 100 shares, or you could purchase a call at 5 and invest only $500. The premium consists of 2 points of intrinsic value and 3 points of time value.

If you buy 100 shares, you are required to pay for the purchase within three business days. If you buy the call, you make payment the following day. The payment deadline for any transaction is called the *settlement date*.

As a call buyer, your plan may be to sell the call prior to expiration. Most call buyers are speculating on price movement in the underlying stock and do not intend to actually exercise the call; rather, their plan is to sell the call at a profit. In the example, a $500 investment gives you control over 100 shares of stock. That's leverage. You do not need to invest and place at risk $6,200 to gain that control. The stock buyer, in comparison, is entitled to receive dividends and does not have to work against the time deadline. Without considering trading costs associated with buying and selling calls, what might happen in the immediate future?

If a 5-point gain occurred by the point of expiration, it would translate to only a 2-point net gain for the option buyer:

Original cost	$500
Less evaporated time value	−300
Original intrinsic value	$200
Plus increased intrinsic value	+500
Value at expiration	$700
Profit	$200

A point-for-point change in option premium value would be substantial. An in-the-money increase of 1 point yields 1.6 percent to the stockholder, but a full 20 percent to the option buyer. If there were to be no price change between purchase and expiration, three-fifths of the option premium would evaporate due to the disappearance of time value. The call buyer risks a loss in this situation even without a change in the stock's market value.

As a call buyer, you are under pressure of time for two reasons. First, the option will expire at a specified date in the future. Second, as expiration approaches, the rate of decline in time value increases, making it even more difficult for options traders to get to breakeven or profit status. At that point, increase in market value of the underlying stock must be adequate to offset time value *and* to yield a profit above striking price in excess of the premium price you paid.

It is possible to buy calls with little or no time value. To do so, you will have to select calls that are relatively close to expiration, so that only a short time remains for the stock's value to increase, and fairly close to striking price to reduce the premium cost. The short time period increases risk in one respect; the lack of time value reduces risk in another respect.

Example

Just a Little Time: In the second week of May, the May 50 call is selling for 2 and the underlying stock is worth 51.50 (1.5 points in the money). You buy one call. By the third Friday (the following week), you are hoping for an increase in the market value of the underlying stock. If the stock were to rise 1 point, the option would be minimally profitable. With only 0.5 point of time value, only a small amount of price movement is required to offset time value and produce in-the-money profits (before considering trading fees). Because time is short, your chances for realizing a profit are limited. But profits, if they do materialize, will be very close to a dollar-for-dollar movement with the stock, given the small amount of time value remaining. If the stock were to increase 3 points, you could double your money in a day or two. And of course, were the stock to drop 2 points or more, the option would become worthless. Considering trading costs, examples of small-point scenarios like this are most realistic for multiple-contract strategies. For example, if you were to buy 10 calls at $51.50, you would invest $510.50 plus trading costs; but on a per-contract basis, trading costs would be far lower than for a single-contract purchase.

Key Point

Short-term call buyers hope for price movement, and they may need only a few points. The risk, of course, is that price movement could go in the wrong direction.

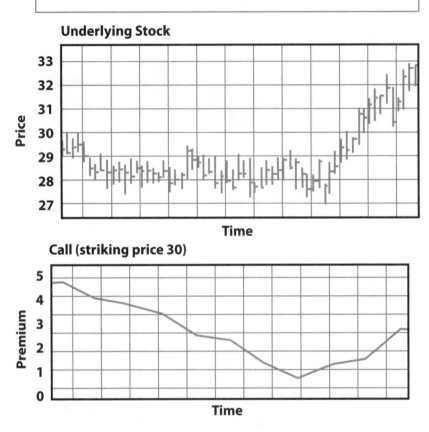

Figure 3.3 Diminishing Time Value of the Call Relative to the Underlying Stock

The greater the time until expiration, the greater the time value premium—and the greater the increase you will require in the market value of the underlying stock, just to maintain the call's value. For the buyer, the interaction between time and time value is the key. This is summarized in Figure 3.3.

Buying calls is one form of leverage—controlling 100 shares of stock for a relatively small investment of capital—and it offers the potential for substantial gain (or loss). But because time value is invariably a factor, the requirements are high. Even with the best timing and analysis of the option and the underlying stock, it is very difficult to earn profits consistently by buying calls.

Strategy 2: Limiting Risks

In one respect, the relatively small investment of capital required to buy a
call *reduces* your risk. A stockholder stands to lose a lot more if and when
the market value of stock declines.

Example

The Lesser of Two Losses: You bought a call two months
ago for a premium of 5. It expires later this month and
is worth nearly nothing, since the stock's market value
has fallen 12 points, well below striking price. You will
lose your $500 investment or most of it, whereas a
stockholder would have lost $1,200 in the same situation.
You controlled the same number of shares for less
exposure to risk, and for a smaller capital investment.
Your loss is always limited to the amount of call premium
paid. This comparison is not entirely valid, however. The
stockholder receives dividends, if applicable, and has the
luxury of being able to hold stock indefinitely. The stock's
market value could eventually rebound. Options traders
cannot afford to wait, because they face expiration in the
near future.

You enjoy the benefits of lower capital exposure only as long as
the option exists. The stockholder has more money at risk but is not
concerned about expiration. It would make no sense to buy calls only
to limit risks, rather than taking the risks of buying shares of stock. A
call buyer believes that the stock will increase in value by expiration
date. Risks are limited in the event that the estimate of near-term price
movement proves to be wrong, but are inapplicable for long-term risk
evaluation.

Strategy 3: Planning Future Purchases

When you own a call, you fix the price of a future purchase of stock in
the event you exercise that call prior to expiration. This use of calls goes
far beyond pure speculation.

In this case, you would have two choices. First, you could sell the call at
18 and realize a profit of $1,500. Second, you could exercise the call and
buy 100 shares of stock at $40 per share. If you seek long-term growth
and believe the stock is a good value, you can use options to freeze the
current price, with the idea of buying 100 shares later.

Example

All a Matter of Timing: The market had a large point drop recently, and one company you have been following experienced a drop in market value. It had been trading in the $50 to $60 range, and you would like to buy 100 shares at the current depressed price of $39 per share. You are convinced that market value will eventually rebound. However, you do not have $3,900 available to invest at the moment. You will be able to raise this money within one year, but you believe that by then, the stock's market value will have returned to its higher range level. Not knowing exactly what will happen, one alternative in this situation is to buy a LEAPS call. To fix the price, you can buy calls while the market is low with the intention of exercising each call once you have the capital available. The 40 LEAPS call expiring in 12 months currently is selling for 3, and you purchase one contract at that price. Six months later, the stock's market price has risen to $58 per share. The call is worth 18 just before expiration. The same strategy—looking ahead one year—would not have been possible with shorter-term listed calls.

The advantage to this strategy is that your market risk is limited. So if you are wrong and the stock continues to fall, you lose only the option premium. If you are right, you pick up 100 shares below market value upon exercise.

Some option speculators recognize that large drops in overall market value are often temporary, as a single-stock reaction to marketwide short-term trends. So a large price drop could represent a buying opportunity, especially in those stocks that fall more than the average marketwide drop. In this situation, investors are likely to be concerned with the risk of further price drops, so they hold off and miss the opportunity. As an options trader, you can afford to speculate on the probability of a price rebound and buy calls. When the market does bounce back, you can sell those calls at a profit.

Strategy 4: Insuring Profits

Another reason for buying calls is to protect a short position in the underlying stock. Calls can be used as a form of insurance. If you have sold short 100 shares of stock, you were hoping that the market value would fall so that you could close out the position by buying 100 shares at a lower market price. The risk, of course, is that the stock will rise in market value, creating a loss for you as a short seller.

Example

Checking Your Shorts: An investor sells short 100 shares of stock when market value is $58 per share. One month later, the stock's market value has fallen to $52 per share. The investor enters a closing purchase transaction—buys 100 shares—and realizes a profit of $600 before trading costs.

A short seller's risks are unlimited in the sense that a stock's market value, in theory at least, could rise to any level. If the market value does rise above the initial sale price, each point represents a point of loss for the short seller. To protect against the potential loss in that event, a short seller can buy calls for insurance.

Example

Reducing Your Risk: You sell short 100 shares when market value is $58 per share. At the same time, you buy one call with a striking price of 65, paying a premium of one-half, or $50. The risk is no longer unlimited. If market value rises above $65 per share, the call protects you; each dollar lost in the stock will be offset by a dollar gained in the call. Risk, then, is limited to 7 points (the difference between the short sale price of $58 and the call's striking price of 65).

In this example, a deep out-of-the-money call was inexpensive, yet it provided valuable insurance for short selling. The protection lasts only until expiration of the call, so if you want to protect the position, the expired call will have to be replaced with another call. This reduces your potential loss through buying offsetting calls, but it also erodes a portion of your profits. As a short seller, like anyone buying insurance, you need to assess the cost of insurance versus the potential risk.

Example

The Need for More: A short seller pays a premium of 2 and buys a call that expires in five months. If the value of the stock decreases 2 points, the short seller might take the profit and close the position; however, with the added cost of the call, a 2-point change represents a breakeven point (before calculating the trading costs). The short seller needs more decrease in market value to create a profit.

Calls serve an important function when used by short sellers to limit risks. They also take part of their potential profit for insurance, so short sellers hope that the strategy will be profitable enough to justify the added expense. Using LEAPS calls in this situation will cost more but provide the same insurance for a longer period of time. The selection of a call to insure a short position depends on the length of time you plan to remain in the short stock position.

Example

The Effect of Rumors: An investor sold short 100 shares of stock at $58 per share. At the same time, he bought a call with a striking price of 65 and paid a premium of 2. A few weeks later, the underlying stock's market price rose on rumors of a pending merger, to a price of $75 per share. The short seller is down $1,700 in the stock (shares were sold at $58 and currently are valued at $75). However, the call is worth $1,000 in intrinsic value plus whatever time value remains. To close the position, the investor can exercise the call and reduce the loss to $700—the sale price of the stock ($58), versus the striking price of the exercised call (65 per share). In this case, an additional call with later expiration and higher striking price could be purchased to continue providing additional insurance. This overall strategy makes sense only if the investor continues to believe that the stock's value will eventually fall and recognizes that the use of calls is a valuable strategy while waiting out the short sale move. If the investor now believes that the stock is not going to fall, then continuing with the short sale in stock would not make sense; the smart move would be to close out the position and take the loss, before a larger loss occurs. Otherwise, if the stock's value continues to rise after the call has been closed, the investor risks further losses.

Strategy 5: Premium Buying

A final strategy involves buying calls to average out the cost of stock held in the portfolio. This is an alternative to *dollar cost averaging* (see Chapter 6). Stockholders who desire to hold shares of a company's stock for the long term may want to buy stock while prices are stable or falling, on the idea that lower prices represent an averaging-down of the overall net price per share. However, the dollar cost averaging strategy, as effective as it is in a declining market situation, is not as desirable when stock prices rise. In that case, hindsight shows that you would have been better off to buy more shares at the original price.

This is a dilemma. If you plan to keep a stock as an investment over the long term, but you do not want to put all your capital into the stock right now (fearing possible decline in value), one alternative is call premium buying. When you purchase a call using this strategy, you seek longer-term out-of-the-money calls for relatively low premium levels. Then, if the stock's value does rise, you can purchase additional shares below market value.

Example

Climbing the Wall of Worry: You own 400 shares of a particular company and you want to buy another 200 to 400 shares in coming months. You originally planned to buy more shares any time the stock's price dropped, creating a lower average cost with each subsequent purchase. However, at the same time you are concerned about losing the opportunity to buy at today's price in the event the stock's price rises. You purchase two calls, one 2 points out of the money expiring in three months, the other 7 points out expiring in six months.

By employing this strategy, you can have it both ways. If the stock's market value falls, you buy additional shares and reduce your overall basis in stock; if the stock's market value rises, you can exercise your calls and fix the stock purchase price at the call striking prices, even if the stock's market value goes far above those levels.

Buying *more* shares of a company whose prospects are increasingly poor is never sensible. However, in utilizing an options strategy such as premium buying in conjunction with downward dollar cost averaging, we assume that the investor has performed the required level of fundamental

analysis to be confident in the company's long-term value.
This has to be offset against the cost of premium buying; you
need to ensure that the money paid for call premium is not
so excessive that the dollar cost averaging advantages are less
than the advantages of simply buying stock at a higher price.

Strategy 6: Pure Speculation

The last popular reason for buying calls is simply to speculate on price
movement of the underlying stock. A speculator hopes the stock will
move upward after the call has been bought because that is the only way
profits will follow. Most speculators lose money on call purchases because
time works against them, so it makes sense to speculate only if you have a
good reason to believe the price of the stock is going to rise.

All time value premium is going to evaporate by expiration date, so the
option premium has to rise enough to offset lost time value and to create
enough intrinsic value to exceed the call's original cost. So if you pay a
total of 4 ($400) and 3 of those points are time value, you need the stock
to rise 3 points above the call's strike price just to break even.

With the problem of time value in mind, you have to pick calls carefully, based on the proximity between striking price and the current price of the stock. The closer the striking price to current price, the higher the extrinsic value is likely to be; and the farther away from expiration, the higher the time value. So the ideal situation involves three attributes:

1. The call's striking price should be close to the current value of the stock.
2. Time to expiration has to be adequate for the stock to have time to make a strong upward move. This is a difficult judgment call.
3. As little extrinsic value as possible should reside in the call's premium. This enables the call's premium to be highly reactive to movement in the stock's price. In some situations, time value is nearly zero because "normal" time value is offset by reduced extrinsic value. This implies that there is little belief that the stock's price will rise in the money by expiration. In some situations, you can find calls with quite a long time until expiration that are nearly all time value, which results from this offset. Normal time value minus negative extrinsic value may create intrinsic value bargains.

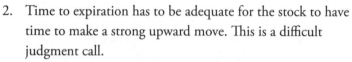

Example

Surfing on Intrinsic Wave: In December 2008, when the auto bailout was in the news, General Motors stock was at $3.66 per share. On December 12, 2008, the January 2010 calls for 2.50 were valued at 1.60. The intrinsic value was 1.16 (3.66 – 2.50), and combined time and extrinsic value was 0.44. Time to expiration was 13 months. This disparity—nearly no time or extrinsic value within the call's premium—is quite unusual. In this situation, it represented the market's pessimism about GM's future, with bankruptcy pending and no good news to report. But as a call speculator, you bought a call for 1.60 ($160) as opposed to buying 100 shares of the stock at $3.66 ($366). This gave you control over 100 shares for more than a full year. Although this was purely a speculative play, it presented a sensible alternative to speculating in the stock itself. In the event the stock value remained low, you would lose only $166. Had you bought the stock, you would have $366 at risk.

DEFINING PROFIT ZONES

Whatever strategy you employ in your portfolio, always be aware of how much price movement is required to create a profit, the risks involved in the strategy, and the range of potential losses to which you are exposed. Throughout the rest of this book, I use illustrations to define the *breakeven price* as well as *profit zone* and *loss zone* for each strategy. See Figure 3.4 for a sample. Note that prices per share are listed at the left in a column, and the various zones are divided according to price levels. (As with all examples, these zones are simplified for illustration purposes, do not allow for the cost of trading, and usually involve single-option trades. Be sure to add brokerage fees to the cost of all transactions in calculating your own breakeven, profit, and loss zones.)

breakeven price

Also called the *breakeven point*; the price of the underlying stock at which the option investor breaks even. For call buyers, this price is the number of points above striking price equal to the call premium cost; for put buyers, this price is the number of points below striking price equal to the put premium cost.

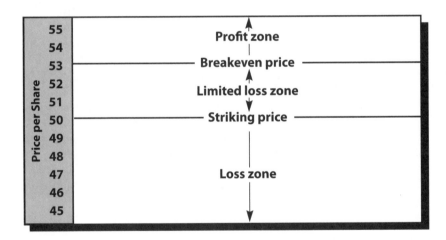

Figure 3.4 A Call's Profit and Loss Zones

In this example, a loss occurs if the option expires out of the money, as is always the case. Because you paid a premium of 3, when the underlying stock's market value is 3 points or less above striking price, the loss will be limited. (Striking price was 50, so if the stock reaches $52, there will be 2 points of intrinsic value at point of expiration, for example.) With limited intrinsic value between striking price and 53, there is not enough increase in market value to produce a profit. Once the stock reaches $53 per share, you are at breakeven, because you are 3 points in the money and you paid 3 for the option. When the stock rises above the $53 per share level, you enter the profit zone.

profit zone

The price range of the underlying stock in which the option investor realizes a profit. For the call buyer, the profit zone extends upward from the breakeven price. For the put buyer, the profit zone extends downward from the breakeven price.

loss zone

The price range of the underlying stock in which the option investor loses. A limited loss exists for option buyers, since the premium cost is the maximum loss that can be realized.

Examples

A Math Quiz: You buy a call and pay a premium of 3, with a striking price of 50. What must the stock's price become by point of expiration, in order for you to break even (not considering trading costs)? What price must the stock achieve in order for a profit to be gained, assuming that only intrinsic value will remain at the time? And at what price will you suffer a loss?

Timing Your Move: You have been tracking a stock with the idea of buying calls. Right now, you could buy a call with a striking price of 40 for a premium of 2. The stock's market value is $38 per share, 2 points out of the money. In deciding whether to buy this call, you understand that between the time of purchase and expiration, the stock will need to rise by no less than 4 points: 2 points to get to the striking price plus 2 more points to cover your cost. If this does occur, the option will be worth exactly what you paid for it, representing a breakeven level (before trading costs). Because the entire premium consists of time value, the stock needs to surpass striking price and develop enough intrinsic value to cover your cost. If price movement were to take place quickly, you could earn a profit consisting of both time and intrinsic value. So the illustration of breakeven and profit zones invariably assumes that all time value will be gone by the time you are ready to close a position.

Defining breakeven price and profit and loss zones helps you to define the range of limited loss in cases such as option buying, so that overall risk can be quantified more easily. An example of a call purchase with defined profit and loss zones is shown in Figure 3.5. In this example, the investor bought one May 40 call for 2. In order to profit from this strategy, the stock's value must increase to a level greater than the striking price of the call plus 2 points (based on the assumption that all time value will have disappeared). So $42 per share is the breakeven price. Even when buying a call scheduled to expire within a few months, you need to know in advance the risks and how much price movement is needed to yield a profit.

Example

Going with Higher Potential: Another stock you have been following has an option available for a premium of 1 and currently is at the money. Expiration is two months away and the stock is only 1 point below breakeven (because of your premium cost). Considering these circumstances, this option has greater potential to become profitable. You need relatively little price movement to create a good profit. If the stock moves adequately at any time in the next two months, you will earn a profit.

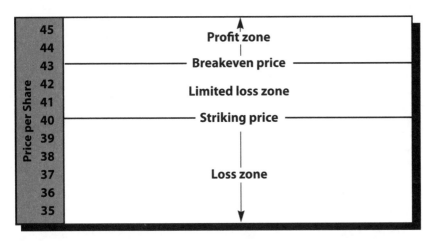

Figure 3.5 Example of Call Purchase with Profit and Loss Zones

In the first example, a breakeven price was 4 points above current market value of the stock, and the option premium was $200. In the second example, only 1 point of price movement is required to reach breakeven. The lower premium also means you are exposed to less potential loss in the event the stock does not rise.

You could make as much profit from a $100 investment as from an equally viable $200 investment, as the previous examples demonstrate. The size of the initial premium cost cannot be used to judge potential profit, whereas it can be used to define potential losses. Premium level can be deceptive, and a more thoughtful risk/reward analysis often is required to accurately compare one option choice to another.

Key Point

The option's premium level cannot be used reliably to judge the viability of a buy decision. It can be used to define potential losses, however.

The calculation of the profit you need and even of the profit zone itself is not always a simple matter. In the previous section, the example of General Motors calls was given to demonstrate that a call with 13 months until expiration consisted almost entirely of intrinsic value. This is a real opportunity for speculation because anything can happen. For example, if the market pessimism about a company were to change suddenly (e.g., if GM got its bailout or its union agreed to drastically change its contracts), then market perspective could change quite rapidly. In this event, two things change. The stock price would rise, of course, but the option premium would adjust as well. This means not only a higher overall premium, but potentially a dramatic increase in extrinsic value.

When prospects for profitable changes in the stock price improve, extrinsic value can change even more rapidly. So the call premium would be likely to rise on the volatility and uncertainty, but also on the increased potential for future price movement. Just as pessimism suppresses extrinsic value unreasonably, optimism is just as likely to exaggerate extrinsic value beyond rational levels.

Another factor to consider when evaluating potential profit is the tax effect of buying options. By definition, a buyer's listed option profits and losses are always short-term because listed stock options expire within one year or less; LEAPS profits may be either short-term or long-term depending on how long the positions are open. So you need to consider the tax consequences of profits as part of the breakeven analysis. The transaction cost also has to be calculated on both sides of the transaction, of course. You probably need to calculate the *after-tax breakeven point*, which is the profit required to break even when also allowing for the federal, state, and (if applicable) local taxes you will owe.

Option profits are taxed in the year a transaction is closed. So option sellers receive payment in one year, but the option may expire or be closed in the following year. In that situation, the option profit is taxed in the latter year, when the option has been closed, exercised, or expires. This raises individual tax planning questions.

Example

A Taxing Matter: You bought a call two months ago
and you want to identify the after-tax breakeven point.
Your effective tax rate (combining federal and state) is 50
percent, so your breakeven cannot simply be restricted
to the calculation of pretax profit. Even though the true
breakeven point is variable (because as you earn more,
a higher amount of tax will be due), you should build
in a 50 percent cushion to the breakeven calculation. If
you were to make $200 on an option transaction, $100
would have to go to pay a combined federal and state
tax liability, so you would have to raise the breakeven by
two more points to create an after-tax breakeven of $200
($400 pretax profit minus $200 tax liability).

The important point to remember about taxes is how that figures into
your overall goal setting. A "profit" is going to be much smaller if your
tax rate is high, and combined federal and state rates can take a significant
share of your pretax profit.

The after-tax breakeven point has to be calculated figuring both federal
and state rates. The only way you can keep 100 percent of your profits is
when you have a carryover loss, which can be deducted only at the rate
of $3,000 per year on your federal return. However, if you have profits
in the current year, you can offset those profits against your unused
carryover losses and shelter current-year profits. These are among the
many considerations to keep in mind when developing a strategy for
buying options.

Before buying any option, evaluate the attributes of the underlying
stock and the profit or loss potential of the option. The analysis of the
underlying stock should include, at a minimum, a study of market price,
dividend history and rate, price volatility, *price/ratio*, earnings history,
and other fundamental and technical features that define a stock's safety
and stability. There is no point to selecting an option that has price
appeal, when the underlying stock has undesirable qualities, such as price
unpredictability, inconsistent financial results, weak position within a
sector or industry, or an inconsistent dividend history. At the very least,
determine from recent history how responsive the stock's market price
is to the general movement of the market. Options cannot be evaluated
apart from their underlying stock, because that would ignore the

important risk attributes of the stock and its potential volatility. The value and profit potential in your options strategy grows from first selecting stock candidates that are a good fit with your own risk profile. It is the wise selection of a range of "good" stocks (by the definition you use to make stock value judgments) that determines viable option selection.

You may also evaluate the entire stock market before deciding whether your timing is good for buying calls. For example, do you believe that the market has been on an upward climb that may require a short-term correction? If so, it is possible that buying options, even on the best stock choices, could be ill timed. No one truly knows how markets will move, or why they behave as they do, even though you may find yourself on a continual quest to find a method to gain such insights. The process of buying and selling is based, invariably, on timing and opinion. See Chapter 8 for a more in-depth and expanded study and discussion of stock selection.

Beyond the point of stock and option analysis, observe the time factor and how the passage of time affects option premium. Time value changes predictably, but in different degrees by stock and from one period to another. Changes in time value can be elusive and unpredictable in the degree and timing. The only certainty is that at expiration, no time value will remain in the option premium.

In the next chapter, strategies for buying puts are examined in depth.

4 BUYING PUTS: THE POSITIVE SIDE OF PESSIMISM

Blessed is he who expects nothing, for he shall never be disappointed.
—Alexander Pope, letter, October 16, 1727

Do you believe the market is headed down? If so, puts could serve as a valuable weapon in your pessimistic market strategy.

Call buyers acquire the right to *buy* 100 shares of an underlying stock. In contrast, a put grants the buyer the opposite right: to sell 100 shares of an underlying stock. Upon exercise of a put, the buyer sells 100 shares at the fixed contract price, even if the stock's current market value has fallen below that level.

It is easy to get confused because calls and puts are opposites. In other words, if the underlying stock's value goes down, the put's value goes up. The put works in the other direction. So buying puts, which can be done for several reasons, is an action you will take if you expect declining stock prices; if you want to protect a long stock position in the event of a decline in price; or when entering a more advanced strategy combining puts with calls—more on this later.

As a put buyer, you have a choice to make in the near future. You may sell the put before it expires; you may exercise the put and sell 100 shares of the underlying stock at the fixed striking price; or you may let the put expire worthless.

You are not obligated to sell 100 shares by virtue of owning the put. That decision is entirely up to you, and is a right but not an obligation. The seller, however, would be obligated to buy 100 shares if you did decide to exercise the put.

Key Point

The buyer of an option always has the right, but not the obligation, to exercise. The seller has no choice in the event of exercise.

As a put buyer, your decisions will depend on the same features that affect and motivate call buyers:

- Price movement in the underlying stock and how that affects the put's premium value.
- Your motives for buying the put, and how today's market conditions meet or do not match those motives.
- Your willingness to wait out a series of events between purchase date and expiration and see what develops, versus your desire for a sure profit in the short term.

Additionally, the same rules apply to puts and to calls regarding the trend in extrinsic value. If you make a distinction between extrinsic and time value, you will recall the important rule: Time value declines over time and is a factor strictly related to the time remaining until expiration. Extrinsic value (usually included as part of time value in a discussion of option valuation) is more complicated.

Extrinsic value, the nonintrinsic portion of option value not related solely to the time element, is affected by numerous things, including:

- *Volatility of the underlying stock.* The more volatile the stock, the greater the related volatility in extrinsic value. This is especially applicable when the stock's price is erratic and chaotic.
- *Trading range of the stock.* A fairly narrow *trading range* tends to hold down extrinsic value, but when a stock's market value moves back and forth within a broader trading range, that will be reflected in greater extrinsic value. (This is not the same as volatility of the underlying stock. A volatile stock is erratic and unpredictable. A broad trading range may remain

predictable but with greater distance between its likely high and low price range.)

- *Breakout from established trading range.* When a stock's price moves above or below an established trading range, option extrinsic value will increase as well. Depending on whether movement means that puts (or calls) go in the money, the increased intrinsic value may also be augmented with greater extrinsic (nontime) value within the same trend.

- *Proximity between current market value of stock and striking price of the put.* When the two are within close proximity, extrinsic value—which you might think of as potential for increased value in the future—will be greater as well. This is especially true when the put is out of the money but the stock's current market value is 3 points or less above the striking price.

- *The time element.* While extrinsic value is distinguished from time value, it is going to vary based on (1) time itself and (2) the other considerations listed here.

THE LIMITED LIFE OF THE PUT

If you believe the underlying stock's market value will decline in the near future, you can take one of three actions in the market: sell short on shares of the stock, sell calls, or buy puts. When you buy a put, your desire is that the underlying stock value will fall below the striking price; the more it falls, the higher your profit. Your belief and hope is opposite that of a call buyer. In that respect, many people view call buyers as optimists and put buyers as pessimists. It is more reasonable when using puts to define yourself as someone who recognizes the cyclical nature of prices in the market, and who believes that a stock is overvalued. Then put buying is sensible for two reasons. First, if you are correct, it may be a profitable decision. Second, buying puts contains much lower risk than short selling stock or call selling.

Your risk is limited to the premium paid for the put. As a put buyer, you face identical risks to those experienced by the call buyer. But when compared to selling short 100 shares of stock, put buyers have far less risk and much less capital requirement. The put buyer does not have to deposit collateral or pay interest on borrowed stock, is not exposed to exercise as a seller would be, and does not face the same risks as the short seller; yet the put buyer can make as much profit. The only disadvantage is the ever-pending expiration date. Time works against the put buyer, and time value premium evaporates with increasing speed as expiration approaches. If the stock's market value declines, but not enough to offset lost time value in the put, you could experience a loss or only break even. The strategy requires price drops adequate to produce a profit.

Compare the various strategies you can employ using shares of stock or options, depending on what you believe will happen in the near-term future to the market value of the underlying stock:

	You believe that the market will:	
Stock strategy	**Rise**	**Fall**
Option strategy (long)	Buy shares (long)	Sell shares (short)
Option strategy (short)	Buy calls	Buy puts
	Sell puts	Sell calls

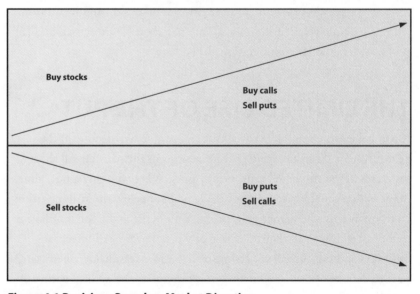

Figure 4.1 Decisions Based on Market Direction

Example

Limiting Risk Exposure: You believe that a particular stock's market value will decline, but you do not want to sell short on the shares, recognizing that the risks and costs are too high. You also do not want to sell a call. That leaves you with a third choice, buying a put. You find a put with several months until expiration, whose premium is 3. If you are right and the stock's market value falls, you could make a profit. But if you are wrong and market value remains the same or rises (or falls, but not enough to produce a profit), your maximum risk exposure is only $300.

As a put buyer, you benefit from a stock's declining market value, and at the same time you avoid the cost and risk associated with short positions. Selling stock short or selling calls exposes you to significant market risks, often for small profit potential.

The limited loss is a positive feature of put buying. However, the put—like the call—exists for only a limited amount of time. To profit from the strategy, you need to see adequate downward price movement in the stock to offset time value and to exceed your initial premium cost. So as a put buyer, you trade limited risk for limited life. If you use long-term equity anticipation security (LEAPS) puts, premium costs will be higher, but you also buy more time; so for some speculators, the LEAPS put is a viable alternative to the short-term listed put.

Key Point

As a put buyer, you eliminate risks associated with going short, and in exchange, you accept the time restrictions associated with option long positions.

The potential benefit to a particular strategy is only half of the equation. The other half is risk. You need to know exactly how much price movement is needed to break even and to make a profit. Given time until expiration, is it realistic to expect that much price movement? There will be greater risks if your strategy requires a 6-point movement in two weeks, and relatively small risks if you need only 3 points of price movement over two months or, in the case of LEAPS, over many more months.

You can view a LEAPS put in terms of risk in one of two ways. Of course, the extrinsic and time value problems and opportunities remain as they do with all options. But the extended period of time has an offsetting element to remember. First, you pay more for the additional time. Second, your risk is reduced because the added time provides more opportunities for favorable price movement. Thus, potential profits are improved for higher initial option premium cost. For anyone purchasing puts, this trade-off is the ultimate judgment call. You seek bargain prices, but you also seek the most time. So the offset between opportunity and risk is defined by the offset between time and cost.

Example

The Time-versus-Cost Decision: You wanted to buy a put on Motorola Solutions (MSI) in the month of April. You reviewed three different possibilities, those expiring in four months (July), in 10 months (January, 2013), and in 22 months (January 2014). At the time, Motorola's market value was $50.39 per share. The put values were:

	Put Striking Prices		
Striking Prices	**4 Months**	**10 Months**	**22 Months**
50	2.56	4.70	7.45
55	5.65	6.70	10.65
60	10.15	15.80	16.35

The selection of one put over another should depend on your preferences: in or out of the money, proximity between striking price and current market value of the stock, and, of course, the price of each put. The 50 put are only slightly out of the money and so the distances between premium value reflect this potential. Extrinsic value is greater, thus the distances between put values based on the proximity issue. But when you study the in-the-money puts (those higher than current market value of $50.39 per share), you can spot some advantageous situations. Extrinsic value again affects the situation; for example, the 55 puts are closer to current market value than the 60s, but study the prices of the 60 puts. These are quite far in the money, considering striking price of 60 and current market value of $50.39—nearly 10 points.

If you were inclined to invest in a long put on this stock and favored in-the-money puts, the 60 is more expensive, but the extrinsic value is very low. If you were to select the 22-month put rather than the 10-month put, the added cost would be only $55, the difference between 15.80 and 16.35. In other words, for only $55, you "buy" an additional 12 months in the put, giving you that extra year of potential. Thus, if Motorola were to decline several points over 22 months, this added cost would provide you with much greater potential for profit. The 55 put can be subjected to the same argument, with the added cost of $395, the difference between 6.70 and 10.65.

The point to this comparison is that the farther away from striking price, the smaller the increments in extrinsic value. This gives you the opportunity to extend the put's lifetime for very little added cost.

Put buying is suitable for you only if you understand the risks and are familiar with price history and volatility in the underlying stock, not to mention the other fundamental and technical aspects that make a particular stock a good prospect for your options strategy. Without a doubt, buying puts is a risky strategy, and the smart put buyer knows this from the start.

STRIKING PRICE

Example

Calling the Market Correctly: You have $600 available and you believe that the market as a whole is overpriced. You expect it to fall in the near future. So you buy two puts at 3 each. The market does fall as expected; but the underlying stock remains unchanged and the puts begin to lose their time value. At expiration, they are worth only 1.

Your perception of the market was correct: Prices fell. But put buyers cannot afford to depend on overall impressions. The strategy lost money because the underlying stock did not behave in the same way as the market in general. The problem with broad market indicators is that such indicators cannot be reliably applied to single stocks. Each stock has its own attributes and reacts differently in changing markets, as well as to its own internal changes—revenues and earnings, capitalization, competitive forces, and the economy, to name a few. Some stocks tend to follow an upward or downward price movement in the larger market, and others do not react to markets as a whole. It is important to study the attributes of the individual stock rather than assuming that overall indicators and index trends are going to apply accurately to a specific stock.

In the preceding example, it appears that the strategy was inappropriate. First, capital was invested in a high-risk strategy. Second, the entire amount was placed into puts on the same stock. By basing a decision on the overall market trend without considering the indicators for the specific company, you lost money. It is likely, too, that you did not understand the degree of price change required to produce a profit. If you do not know how much risk a strategy involves, then it is not an appropriate strategy. More study and analysis is required.

Key Point

When it comes to market risk, the unasked question can lead to unexpected losses. Whatever strategy you employ, you need to first explore and understand all the risks involved.

It is not unusual for investors to concentrate on potential gain without also considering the potential loss, especially in the options market. In the previous example, one reason you lost was a failure to study the individual stock. One aspect not considered was the company's strength in a declining market, its ability to hold its price. This information might have been revealed with more focused analysis and a study of the stock's price history in previous markets. Options traders may lose not because their perception of the market is wrong, but because there was not enough time for their strategy to work—in other words, because they did not fully understand the stock-specific implications and option-specific timing aspects of the decision.

Once you understand the risks and are convinced that you can afford the losses that could occur, you might decide that it is appropriate to buy puts in some circumstances. Remember, though, that the evaluation has to involve not only the option—premium level, time value, and time until expiration—but also the attributes of the underlying stock.

You are aware of the difference between long-term investment and short-term speculation in the preceding example. You have established a base in your portfolio, and you thoroughly understand how the market works. You can afford some minor losses with capital set aside purely for speculation. Buying puts is an appropriate strategy given your belief about the market, particularly since you understand that stocks in your portfolio are likely to fall along with broader market trends. Your ability to afford losses, and the proper selection of stocks on which to buy puts, add up to a greater chance of success.

SHORT-TERM SPECULATION

LONG-TERM SPECULATION

BUYING PUTS

Example

Losses You Can Afford: You are an experienced investor and you have a well-diversified investment portfolio. You own shares in companies in different market sectors and you also own shares in two mutual funds, plus some real estate. You have been investing for several years, fully understand the risks in these markets, and consider yourself a long-term and conservative investor. In selecting stocks, you have always used their potential for long-term price appreciation and a history of stability in earnings as your primary selection criteria. Short-term price movement does not concern you with these longer-term aspects in mind. Outside of this portfolio, you have funds available that you use for occasional speculation. You believe the market will fall in the short term, including the value of shares of stock that you own. You buy puts with this in mind. Your theory: Any short-term losses in your permanent portfolio will be offset by gains in your put speculation. And if you are wrong, you can afford the losses.

JUDGING THE PUT

Time works against all option buyers. Not only will your option expire within a few months, but time value will decline even if the stock's price does not change. Buyers need to offset lost time value with price movement that creates intrinsic value in its place.

You can select low-priced puts—ones that are out of the money—but that means you require many points of price movement to produce a profit. In other words, those puts are low-priced for a good reason. The likelihood of gain is lower than it is for higher-priced puts. When you buy in-the-money puts, you will experience a point-for-point change in intrinsic value; but that can happen in either direction. For put buyers, a downward movement in the stock's market value is offset point for point with gains in the put's premium; but each upward movement in the stock's market value is also offset, by a decline in the put's intrinsic value.

The problem is not limited to picking the right direction a stock's market value might change, although many novice options traders fall into the trap of believing that this is true. Rather, the *degree* of movement within a limited period of time must be adequate to produce profits that exceed premium cost and offset time value (and to cover trading costs on both sides of the transaction). This time-related problem exists for LEAPS puts as well. However, with much longer time involved, many put buyers view the normal market cycles as advantageous even when speculating. For example, you may need to spend more premium dollars to acquire a LEAPS put, but with up to three years until expiration, you will also have many more opportunities to realize a profit.

Examples

A Losing Proposition: You bought a put and paid a premium of 5. At the time, the stock's market value was 4 points below the striking price. It was 4 points in the money. (For calls, "in the money" means the stock's market value is higher than striking price, but the opposite for puts.) However, by expiration, the stock has risen 4.50 points and the option is worth only 0.50 ($50). The time value has disappeared and you sell on the day of expiration, losing $450.

Time Running Out: You bought a put several months ago, paying a premium of 0.50 ($50). At that time, the stock's market value was 5 points out of the money. By expiration, the stock's market value has declined 5.50 points, so that the put is 0.50 point in the money. When you bought the put, it had no intrinsic value and only 0.50 point of time value. At expiration, the time value is gone and there remains only 0.50 point of intrinsic value. Overall, the premium value has not changed, but no profit is possible because the stock's market value did not decline enough.

Whether using listed options or LEAPS to buy puts, it remains a speculative move to go long when time value is involved. Some speculators attempt to bargain hunt in the options market. The belief is that it is always better to pick up a cheap option than to put more money into a high-priced one. This is not always the case; cheap options are cheap because they are *not* necessarily good bargains, and this is widely recognized by the market overall. The question of quality has to be remembered at all times when you are choosing options and comparing prices. The idea of value is constantly being adjusted for information about the underlying stock, but these adjustments are obscured by the double effect of (1) time to go until expiration and the effect on time

value, and (2) distance between current market value of the stock and
the striking price of the option. When the market value of the stock is
close to the striking price, it creates a situation in which profits (or losses)
can materialize rapidly. At such times, the proximity between market
and striking price will also be reflected in option premium. It's true that
lower-priced puts require much less price movement to produce profits;
but these low-priced puts remain long shots.

Key Point

A bargain price might reflect either a bargain or a lack of value
in the option. Sometimes, real bargains are found in higher-
priced options.

Example

Fast Profits: You bought a put last week when it was
in the money, paying a premium of 6. You believed the
stock was overpriced and was likely to fall. Two days after
your purchase, the stock's market value fell 2 points. You
sold the put and received $800. This represents a return
on your investment of 33.3 percent in two days (not
considering trading costs).

In this example, you turned the position around rapidly and walked away with a profit. So the bargain existed in this put because you were right. The return was substantial, but that does not mean that the experience can be repeated consistently. Remember, when you buy puts on speculation, you are gambling that you are right about *short-term* price changes. You might be right about the general trend in a stock but not have enough time for your prediction to become true before expiration. With this in mind, it is crucial to set goals for yourself, knowing in advance when you will sell a put—based on profit goals as well as loss bailout points.

Example

Know When to Quit: You bought a put several months ago, paying a premium of 0.50 ($50). At that time, the stock's market value was 5 points out of the money. By expiration, the stock's market value has declined 5.50 points, so that the put is 0.50 point in the money. When you bought the put, it had no intrinsic value and only 0.50 point of time value. At expiration, the time value is gone and there remains only 0.50 point of intrinsic value. Overall, the premium value has not changed, but no profit is possible because the stock's market value did not decline enough.

Setting goals is the only way to succeed if you plan to speculate by buying options. Too many speculators fall into a no-win trap because they program themselves to lose; they do not set standards, so they do not know when or how to make smart decisions.

Example

Missed Opportunities: You bought a LEAPS put last month and paid 5. With 26 months to go before expiration, you thought there was plenty of time for a profit to materialize. Your plan was to sell if the value went up 2 points. A month after your purchase, the stock's market value fell and the put's value went up to 8, an increase of 3 points. You did not sell, however, because you thought the stock's market value might continue to fall. If that happened and the put's value increased, you did not want to lose out on future profits. But the following week, the stock's value rebounded 4 points, and the put followed, losing 4 points. The opportunity was lost. This pattern repeated several times and the put ended up worthless at the point of expiration.

This example demonstrates the absolute need for firm goals. Even with a lot of time, you cannot expect to realize a profit unless you also know when to close the position. Inexperienced option speculators do not recognize the need to take profits when they are there, or to cut losses—either decision based on a predetermined standard. When the put becomes more valuable, human nature tells us, "I could make even more money if I wait." When the put's value falls, the same voice says, "I can't sell now. I have to get back to where I started."

Ask yourself: If you listen to that voice, when do you sell? The answer, of course, is that you can never sell. Whether your option is more valuable or less valuable, the voice tells you to wait and see. Lost opportunities are unlikely to repeat themselves, given the time factor associated with options; and even when those opportunities

do reappear with a LEAPS put, it does not mean that the right decision will be made. The old stock market advice, "Buy in a rising market," cannot be applied to options, because options expire. Not only that, but time value declines, which means that profits you gain in intrinsic value could be offset if you wait too long. You need to take profits or cut losses at the right moment.

Example

Hesitate–and Lose: You bought a put last month for 6, and resolved that you would sell if its value rose or fell by 2 points. Two weeks ago, the stock's market value rose 2 points and the put declined to your bailout level of 4. You hesitated, hoping for a recovery. Today, the stock has risen a total of 5 points since you bought the put, which is now worth 1.

In this example, you would lose $300 by not following your own standard and bailing out at 4. Even if the stock did fall later on, time would work against you. The longer it takes for a turnaround in the price of the underlying stock, the more time value loss you need to overcome. The stock might fall a point or two over a three-month period, so that you merely trade time value for intrinsic value, with the net effect of zero; it is even likely that the overall premium value will decline if intrinsic value is not enough to offset the lost time value.

The problem of time value deterioration is the same problem experienced by call buyers. It does not matter whether price movement is required to go up (for call buyers) or down (for put buyers); time is the enemy, and price movement has to be adequate to offset time value as well as produce a profit through more intrinsic value. If you seek bargains several points away from the striking price, it is easy to overlook this reality. You need a substantial change in the stock's market value just to arrive at the price level where intrinsic value will begin to accumulate. The relationship between the underlying stock and time value premium is illustrated in Figure 4.2.

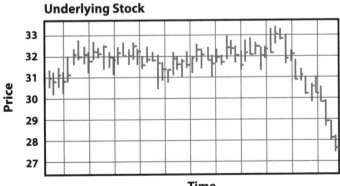

Call (striking price 30)

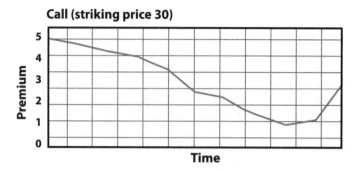

Figure 4.2 Diminishing Time Value of the Put Relative to the Underlying Stock

Example

Good Trend but Not Enough: You bought a LEAPS put for 5 with a striking price of 30, when the stock was at $32 per share. There were 22 months to go until expiration and the entire put premium was time value; you estimated that there was plenty of time for the price of the stock to fall, producing a profit. Between purchase date and expiration, the underlying stock falls to 27, which is 3 points in the money. At expiration, the put is worth 3, meaning you lose $200 on sale of the put. Time value has evaporated. Even though you are 3 points in the money, it is not enough to match or beat your investment of $500.

The farther out of the money, the cheaper the premium for the option—and the lower the potential to realize a profit. Even using LEAPS and depending on longer time spans, you have to accept the reality: The current time value premium reflects the time until expiration, so you will pay more time value premium for longer-term puts. That means you have to overcome more points to replace time value with intrinsic value.

If you buy an in-the-money put and the underlying stock increases in value, you lose one point for each dollar of increase in the stock's market value—as long as it remains in the money—and for each dollar lost in the stock's market value, your put gains a point in premium value. Once the stock's market value rises above striking price, there remains no intrinsic value; your put is out of the money and the premium value becomes less responsive to price movement in the underlying stock. While all this is going on, time value is evaporating as well.

Key Point

For option buyers, profits are realized primarily when the option is in the money. Out-of-the-money options are poor candidates for appreciation, because time value rarely increases.

Whether you prefer lower-premium, out-of-the-money puts or higher-premium in-the-money puts, always be keenly aware of the point gap between the stock's current market value and striking price of the put. The further out of the money, the less likely it is that your put will produce a profit.

To minimize your exposure to risk, limit your speculation to options on stocks whose market value is within 5 points of the striking price. In other words, if you buy out-of-the-money puts, avoid those that are deep out of the money. What might seem like a relatively small price gap can become quite large when you consider that all the out-of-the-money premium is time value, and that no intrinsic value can be accumulated until your put goes in the money. Added to this problem is the time factor. As shown in Figure 4.3, you may want to avoid speculating in puts that are either deep in the money or deep out of the money. Deep-in-the-

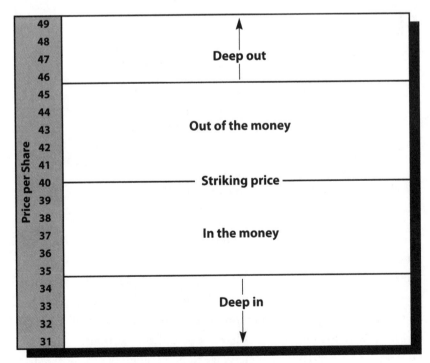

Figure 4.3 Deep-In/Deep-Out Stock Prices for Puts

money puts are going to be expensive—one point for each dollar below striking price, plus time value—and deep-out-of-the-money puts are too far from striking price to have any realistic chances for producing profits.

PUT BUYING STRATEGIES

There are three reasons to buy puts. The first is purely speculative: the hope of realizing a profit in a short period of time, with relatively small risk exposure. This leveraged approach is appealing but contains higher risks along with the potential for short-term profits. The second reason to buy puts is as an alternative to short selling of stock. And third, you may buy puts to provide yourself with a form of insurance against price declines in a stock long position.

Strategy 1: Gaining Leverage

There is value in the leverage gained using the put. With a limited amount of capital, the potential for profits is greater for put buyers than through stock short selling, and with considerably less risk.

Example

Safer than Shorting Stock: A stock currently is valued at $60 per share. If you sell short 100 shares and the stock drops 5 points, you can close the position and take a profit of $500. However, rather than selling short, you could buy 12 puts at 5, for a total investment of $6,000. A 5-point drop in this case would produce a profit of $6,000, a 100 percent gain (assuming no change in time value). So by investing the same amount in puts, you could earn a 100 percent profit, compared to an 8.3 percent profit through short selling.

This example demonstrates the value in leverage, but the risk element for each strategy is not comparable. The short seller faces risks not experienced by the put buyer and has to put up collateral and pay interest; in comparison, the put buyer has to fight against time. Risking $6,000 by buying puts is highly speculative and, while short selling is risky as well, the two strategies have vastly different attributes. The greater profit potential through leverage in buying puts is accompanied by equally higher risk of loss. However, even without a large sum of capital to speculate with, you can still use leverage to your advantage. This comparative analysis shows the flaw in analyzing two dissimilar strategies. Because the risk attributes are so different for each, it is not accurate to draw conclusions based only on potential returns.

LEVERAGE

Example

Comparing Apples to Oranges: You buy a LEAPS put for 5 with a striking price of 60 and 18 months until expiration. The stock currently is selling at $60 per share; your option is at the money. Aware of the potential profit or loss in your strategy, your decision to buy puts was preferable over selling short the stock. The luxury of 18 months in the LEAPS put is preferable over remaining exposed to short selling of stock. As shown in Figure 4.4, a drop of 5 points in the stock's market value would produce a $500 gain with either strategy (assuming no change in time value premium).

The short seller, like the put buyer, has a time problem. The short seller has to place collateral on deposit equal to a part of the borrowed stock's value, and pay interest on the borrowed amount. Thus, the more time the short position is left open, the higher the interest cost—and the more decline in the stock's value the short seller requires to make a profit.

While the put buyer is concerned with diminishing time value, the short seller pays interest, which erodes future profits, if they ever materialize, or increases losses.

A decline of 5 points in the preceding example produces an 8.1 percent profit for the short seller and a 100 percent profit for the put buyer. Compare the risks with this yield difference in mind. Short-selling risks are unlimited in the sense that a stock's value could rise indefinitely, creating ever-increasing losses. The put buyer's risk is limited to the $500 investment. A drop of $1 per share in the stock's value creates a 1.6 percent profit for the short seller, and a 20 percent profit for the put buyer.

Potential losses can be compared between strategies as one form of risk evaluation. When a short seller's stock rises in value, the loss could be substantial. It combines market losses with continuing interest expense and tied-up collateral (creating a lost opportunity). The put buyer's losses can never exceed the premium cost of the put.

	Stock[1]		Put[2]	
	Profit or Loss	**Rate of Return**	**Profit or Loss**	**Rate of Return**
Price decrease of 5 points	$500	8.1%	$500	100%
Price decrease of 1 point	$100	1.6%	$100	20%
No price change	0	0	0	0
Price increase of 1 point	–$100	–1.6%	–$100	–20%
Price increase of 5 points	–$500	–8.1%	–$500	–100%
[1]Sold short at $62 per share ($6,200). [2]Striking price 60, premium 5 ($500).				

Figure 4.4 Rates of Return: Selling Short versus Buying Puts

Strategy 2: Limiting Risks

It is possible to double your money in a very short period of time by speculating in puts. Leverage increases even a modest investment's overall potential (and risk). Risks increase through leverage due to the potential for loss. Like all forms of investing or speculating, greater opportunity also means great risk.

Example

Profits Becoming Unlikely: You recently bought a put for 4. However, expiration date is coming up soon and the stock's market value has risen above striking price. When the put expires, you face the prospect of losing the entire $400 premium. Time has worked against you. Knowing that the stock's market value might eventually fall below striking price, but not necessarily before expiration, you realize it is unlikely that you will be able to earn a profit.

Risks are lower for puts in comparison to short selling. A short seller in a loss position is required to pay the difference between short-sold price and current market value if the stock has risen in value, not to mention the interest cost. The limited risk of buying puts is a considerable advantage.

Example

Big Problems or Small: You sold short 200 shares of stock with market value of $45 per share; you were required to borrow $9,000 worth of stock, put up a portion as collateral, and pay interest to the brokerage company. The stock later rose to $52 per share and you sold. Your loss on the stock was $1,400 plus interest expense. If you had bought puts instead, the maximum loss would have been limited to the premium paid for the two puts. The fear of further stock price increases that would concern you as a short seller would be a minimal problem for you as a put buyer.

The advantage enjoyed by the put buyer typifies the long position over the short position. Losses are invariably limited in this situation. Although both strategies have the identical goal, risks make the long and short positions much different.

Strategy 3: Hedging a Long Position

Put buying is not always merely speculative. You can also buy one put for every 100 shares of the underlying stock owned, to protect yourself against the risk of falling prices. Just as calls can be used to insure against the risk of rising prices in a short sale position, puts can serve the same purpose, protecting against price declines when you are long in shares of stock. When a put is used in this manner, it is called a *married put*, since it is tied directly to the underlying stock.

This strategy is also one form of a *synthetic position*. The use of a long put with long stock creates a synthetic call. (When you use a long call to protect your position with short stock, it is called a synthetic put.) The risk of declining market value is a constant concern for every investor. If you buy stock and its value falls, a common reaction is to sell in the fear that the decline will continue. In spite of advice to the contrary, you may have sold low and bought high. It is human nature. It requires a cooler head to calmly wait out a decline and rebound, which could take months, even years. Special tax rules apply to married puts, so, in calculating the cost and benefit to this strategy, you also need to evaluate the tax status for your stock.

The married put is a form of insurance protection. This strategy makes sense, whether you end up selling the appreciated put or exercising it. In the event of a decline in the stock's value, you have the right to exercise and sell the stock at the striking price. However, if you believe the stock remains a sound investment, it is preferable to offset losses by selling the put at a profit. When you exercise a put, that action is referred to as *put to seller*.

married put

The status of a put used to hedge a long position. Each put owned protects 100 shares of the underlying stock held in the portfolio. If the stock declines in value, the put's value will increase and offset the loss.

synthetic position

A strategy in which stock and option positions are matched up to protect against unfavorable price movement. When you own stock and also buy a put to protect against downward price movement, it creates a synthetic call. When you are short on stock and buy a call, it creates a synthetic put.

Example

A Profitable Dilemma: You own 100 shares of stock that you purchased for $57 per share. This stock tends to be volatile, meaning the potential for short-term gain or loss is significant. To protect yourself against possible losses, you buy a put on the underlying stock. It costs 1 and has a striking price of 50. Two months later, the stock's market value falls to $36 per share and the put is near expiration. The put has a premium value of 14.

put to seller

Action of exercising a put and requiring the seller to purchase 100 shares of stock at the fixed striking price.

In this situation, you have two choices:

1. Sell the put and take the $1,300 profit. Your adjusted cost was $58 per share (purchase price of $5,700 plus $100 for the put). Your net cost per share is $44 ($5,700 less $1,300 profit on the put). Your basis now is 8 points above current market value. By selling the put, you have the advantage of continuing to own the stock. If its market value rebounds to a level above $44 per share, you will realize a profit. Without

the put, your basis would be 21 points above current market value. Selling the put eliminates a large portion of the loss.

2. Exercise the put and sell the stock for $50 per share. In this alternative, you sell at 8 points below your basis. You lose $100 paid for the put, plus 7 points in the stock.

Regardless of the choice taken in these circumstances, you end up with a smaller loss by owning the married put than you would have only owning the stock. The put either cuts the loss by offsetting the stock's market value decline, or enables you to get rid of the depreciated stock at higher than market value. You have a loss either way, but not as much of a loss as you would have had without buying the put.

The married put in this application provides you with *downside protection*, which reduces potential profits because you have to pay a premium to buy the insurance. If you intend to own shares of stock for the long term, puts will have to be replaced upon expiration, so that the cost is repetitive. However, as a long-term investor, you are not normally concerned with short-term price change, so the strategy is best employed only when you believe your shares currently are overpriced, given the rate of price change and current market conditions. In this situation, using puts for insurance is speculative but may remain a prudent choice.

In the event the stock's market price rises, your potential losses are frozen at the level of the put's premium and no more. This occurs because as intrinsic value in the put declines, it is offset by a rise in the stock's market value. Whether you end up selling the put or exercising, downside protection establishes an acceptable level of loss in the form of insurance, and fixes that loss at the striking price of the put, at least for the duration of the put's life. This strategy is appropriate even when, as a long-term investor, you expect instability in the market in the short term.

A summary of the insurance strategy is shown in Figure 4.5. Note that regardless of the severity of decline in the stock's market value, the loss can never exceed 4.8 percent of the total amount invested (the cost of the put). That is because for every point of decline in the stock's market value, the put increases one point in intrinsic value. This status continues until the put expires.

downside protection

A strategy involving the purchase of one put for every 100 shares of the underlying stock that you own. This insures you against losses to some degree. For every in-the-money point the stock falls, the put will increase in value by one point. Before exercise, you may sell the put and take a profit, offsetting stock losses, or exercise the put and sell the shares at the striking price.

Price Movement, Underlying Stock	Profit or Loss		Net Profit or Loss[3]	
	Stock[1]	Put[2]	Amount	Rate
Down 20 points	–$2,000	$1,700	–$ 300	– 4.8%
Down 5 points	–$ 500	–$ 200	–$ 300	– 4.8%
Down 3 points	–$ 300	0	–$ 300	– 4.8%
No change	0	–$ 300	–$ 300	– 4.8%
Up 3 points	$ 300	–$ 300	0	0
Up 5 points	$ 500	–$ 300	$ 200	3.2%
Up 20 points	$2,000	–$ 300	$1,700	27.0%

[1] Stock purchased at $60 per share.
[2] Put striking price 60, premium 3.
[2] Return based on total cost of $6,300.

Figure 4.5 Downside Protection: Buying Shares and Buying Puts

Example

Damage Assessment: You recently bought 100 shares of stock at $60 per share. At the same time, you bought a put with a striking price of 60, paying 3. Your total investment is $6,300. Before making your purchase, you analyzed the potential profit and loss and concluded that your losses would probably not exceed 4.8 percent ($300 paid for the put, divided by $6,300, the total invested). You also concluded that an increase in the stock's market value of 3 points or less would not represent a profit at all, due to the investment in the put. So profits will not begin to accumulate until the stock's market value exceeds $63 per share.

The insurance strategy is also a powerful tool when you plan to sell stock within the next three years, and you are concerned about the potential for losses by that deadline. Insurance protects your value and ensures that, even if the stock's value declines dramatically, you will not lose by continuing to own the stock.

Example

A Wise Financial Planning Move: Several years ago you invested in 1,000 shares of stock and it has appreciated consistently over the years. You are planning to sell the stock in two years and use the funds as a down payment on a home. You don't want to sell the stock until the money is needed, for several reasons. You will be taxed on profits in the year sold, so you want to defer that until the latest possible moment. In addition, you would prefer to continue earning dividends and, potentially, additional profits in the stock. But you also know the stock's value could fall. Even a temporary decline would be serious because you will need those funds at a specific date in the future. The solution: Buy 10 puts to insure the value at the striking price. Select puts with expiration dates at or beyond your target date. This reduces your stock's value by the cost of the puts, but it also ensures that any in-the-money declines in the stock's price will be offset by gains in the puts' value.

In this case, the decision to use puts is not merely speculative; it is necessary to insure the stock's market value. A decline might be reversed within 6 to 12 months, but that could create a hardship if you have a specific date in mind to buy a house. The use of puts as insurance can be applied in many ways to protect capital invested in stocks. Even the best stocks can experience a price decline in cyclical markets. When you cannot afford even a temporary decline, puts can be used to lock in a striking price value.

Strategy 4: Pure Speculation

Just as call buyers speculate on a stock's price rising, put buyers accomplish the same result with puts. However, put buyers are hoping that the underlying stock's price will move downward.

The rules for comparison between intrinsic, extrinsic, and time value are identical for puts and for calls, but with underlying price movement taking place in the opposite direction. So the more a stock's price falls, the higher the premium value in the put.

Market sentiment plays a big role in determining the level of extrinsic value, of course. If the perception about a company is that its future is bleak, put value is likely to hold greater extrinsic value, notably for puts with a long duration remaining until expiration. However, if the optimistic view prevails and the perception is that the stock price will move upward, then put extrinsic values are likely to decline.

In selecting the best puts for speculation, three criteria should be in place, including:

1. The put's striking price should be close to the current value of the stock.

Example

Putting the Matter to Rest: You have been watching a stock rise over the past month on what you consider overly optimistic outlooks for the company's future. This includes a rumor that the company is a takeover candidate, which you do not believe. The rise in price has recently stalled and you expect the price to fall in coming weeks. You pick a put and buy it. The strike is slightly lower than current market value, which means the premium cost is quite low. You anticipate a fast change in the stock's price, so you are less concerned with time value decline than you normally would be; if the stock's price falls as you expect, the long put could become profitable very quickly.

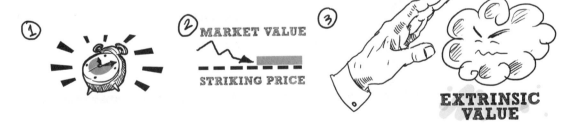

2. Time to expiration has to be adequate for the stock to have time to make a strong downward move. This is a difficult judgment call.

3. As little extrinsic value as possible should reside in the put's premium. This enables the put's premium to be highly reactive to downward movement in the stock's price. Otherwise, increases in intrinsic value will be offset by a decline in previously inflated extrinsic value, making it difficult to realize profits from put buying.

DEFINING PROFIT ZONES

To decide whether buying puts is a reasonable strategy for you, always be aware of potential profits and losses, rather than concentrating on profits alone. Comparing limited losses to potential profits when using puts for downside protection is one type of analysis that helps you pick value when comparing puts. And when looking for a well-priced speculative move, time to expiration coupled with the gap between current market value and striking price—which dictates the amount of time value premium—will help you to find real bargains in puts. Premium level is not a reasonable criterion for your selection.

The profit and loss zones for puts are the reverse of the zones for call buyers, because put owners anticipate a downward movement in the stock, whereas call buyers expect upward price movement. See Figure 4.6 for a summary of loss and profit zones and breakeven point using the following example.

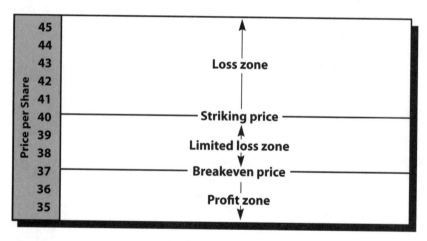

Figure 4.6 A Put's Profit and Loss Zones

Example

Cancelling Out the Losses: You buy a put with a striking price of 50, paying 3. Your breakeven price is $47 per share. If the underlying stock falls to that level, the option will have intrinsic value of 3 points, equal to the price you paid for the put. If the price of stock goes below $47 per share, the put will be profitable point for point with downward price movement in the stock. Your put can be sold when the underlying stock's market value is between $47 and $50 per share, for a limited loss. And if the price of the stock rises above $50 per share, the put will be worthless at expiration.

Before buying any put, determine the profit and loss zones and breakeven price (including the cost of trading on both sides of the transaction). For the amount of money you will be putting at risk, how much price movement will be required to produce a profit? How much time remains until expiration? Is the risk a reasonable one?

Another example of a put purchase with defined profit and loss zones is shown in Figure 4.7. In this example, the put was bought at 3 and has a May 40 expiration. The outcome of this transaction would be exactly opposite for the purchase of a call, given the same premium, expiration, and price of the underlying stock. You will gain a profit if the stock falls below the breakeven point of 37 (40 strike less 3 premium).

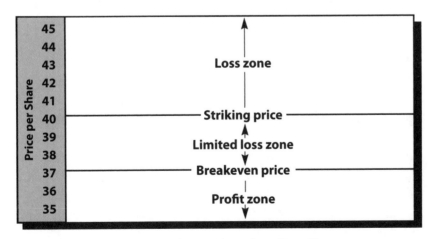

Figure 4.7 Example of Put Purchase with Profit and Loss Zones

Remember this rule: As a buyer, don't depend on time value to produce profits between purchase date and expiration because that is highly unlikely to occur. If you do not experience a price decline in the stock's price adequate to exceed the price you paid for the put, then you will have a loss. Like call purchasing, time works against you when you buy puts. The greater the gap between market price of the stock and striking price, the more time problem you will have to overcome.

The mistake made by many investors is failing to recognize what is required to produce a profit, and failing to analyze a situation to determine whether buying puts makes sense. Analyze these points in evaluating put buying:

- Your motive (leverage, reduction of risk, or downside protection).
- The premium level and amount of time value premium.
- Time remaining until expiration.
- The gap between the stock's current market value and the put's striking price.
- The number of points of movement in the underlying stock required before you can begin earning a profit.
- The characteristics of the underlying stock (see Chapter 8 for guidelines for selecting stocks appropriate for your option strategy).

Collectively, these guidelines define an investment strategy and work for you as tools for evaluating risks and identifying profit potential. You could earn substantial short-term profits; you also face a corresponding high risk level represented by time, the buyer's enemy.

On the opposite side of the option transaction is the seller. Unlike buyers, sellers have an advantage with pending expiration. Time is the seller's friend, and higher time value represents an opportunity rather than a risk. Because time value declines as expiration approaches, the seller benefits in the same degree as the buyer is penalized. You can purchase puts or sell calls and achieve the same strategic position, but the risks may be far different. Calls offer some interesting strategic possibilities for sellers, both high risk and very conservative. The next chapter examines strategies and risks of selling calls.

140

CHAPTER 5

SELLING CALLS: CONSERVATIVE AND PROFITABLE

Strategic planning is worthless—unless there is first a strategic vision.
—John Naisbitt, *Megatrends*, 1984

One of the more interesting aspects of options is that they can be extremely speculative and risky, or the most conservative of strategies. It all depends on whether you are a buyer or a seller, and on whether you own the underlying stock.

The idea of going short—selling first, and buying to close later—is a tough idea to grasp. Most of us think about investing in a precise sequence. First, you buy a security; then, at a later date, you sell. If the sale price is higher than the purchase price, you earn a profit; if it is lower, you suffer a loss. However, when you are a call seller, this sequence is reversed.

By starting out the sequence with an opening sale transaction, you are paid the premium at the time the order is placed. You will pay a purchase price later when you close the position or, if the option expires worthless, you never pay at all. In that case, the entire sale premium is yours to keep as profit. If this all sounds like a pretty good deal, you also need to remember that taking a short position is accompanied by inevitable risks. These risks are explained in this chapter and demonstrated through examples. Some types of call selling are extremely high risk and others are very low risk and conservative.

Key Point

Sellers receive payment when they initiate the opening transaction. That is compensation for accepting exposure to the risks.

Call sellers enjoy significant advantages over call buyers. In the previous two chapters, many examples demonstrated how time value works against the buyer; in fact, the time value premium makes it very difficult for buyers to earn profits with options; the odds are against them. The problem of declining time value is the primary risk of option buying. Even when the underlying stock's market value moves in the desired direction, it might not happen soon enough or with enough point value to offset the time value premium. This buyer's disadvantage is the seller's advantage.

Because time value evaporates, buyers see time as the enemy. For sellers, though, time is a great ally. The more time value involved, the higher the potential profit; and the more that time value falls, the better. When you enter the order for an opening sale transaction, you are better off if you have the maximum time value possible. While buyers seek options with the lowest possible time value and with the stock's market value within reasonable proximity to striking price, sellers do the opposite. They seek calls with the highest possible time value and the largest possible gap between striking price of the option and market value of the stock.

Key Point

Time is the buyer's enemy, but the opposite is true for the seller. The seller makes a profit as time value evaporates.

When you sell a call, you grant the buyer the right to buy 100 shares of the underlying stock at the striking price, at any time prior to expiration. That means that you assume the risk of being required to sell 100 shares of the underlying stock to the buyer, potentially at a striking price far below current market value. The decision to exercise is the buyer's, and that decision can be made at any time. Of course, as long as the call is out of the money, it will not be exercised. That risk becomes real only if and when the call goes in the money (when the stock's market value is higher than the call's striking price).

Example

Stuck with the Strike: You sold a call two months ago with a striking price of 50. At the time the stock's market value was $46 per share. At the beginning of this week, the stock had risen to $58 per share and the buyer exercised your call. You are required to deliver 100 shares at $50 per share. If you own 100 shares of stock, you relinquish ownership and receive $50 per share rather than current market value of $58. If you do not own 100 shares, your brokerage firm will complete the transaction and deduct the difference from your account, or $800 ($58 per share current market value less striking price of $50 per share). Transaction fees will also apply.

All investment strategies contain specific risk characteristics, and these should be clearly identified and fully understood by anyone undertaking the strategy. The risks tend to have unchanging attributes. For example, the risks of buying stocks are consistent from one moment to another. The experienced stock market investor understands this and accepts the risk. However, call selling has a unique distinction. It can be extremely risky or extremely conservative, depending on whether you also own 100 shares of the stock at the time you sell the call.

SELLING UNCOVERED CALLS

When call selling is reviewed in isolation, it is indeed a high-risk strategy. If you sell a call but you do not own 100 shares of the underlying stock, the option is classified as a *naked option* or *uncovered option*. You are exposing yourself to an unlimited risk. In fact, call selling in this situation is one of the most risky strategies you could take, containing high potential for losses. A buyer's risks are limited to the premium cost; depending on how many points a stock moves up, a call seller's losses can be much higher.

When you take a short position in a call, the decision to exercise belongs to the buyer. You need to be able and willing to deliver 100 shares in the event that the call is exercised, no matter how high current market value has gone. If you do not already own 100 shares, you will

naked option

An option sold in an opening sale transaction when the seller (writer) does not own 100 shares of the underlying stock.

uncovered option

The same as a naked option—the sale of an option not covered, or protected, by the ownership of 100 shares of the underlying stock.

be required upon exercise to buy 100 shares at current market value and deliver them at the striking price of the call. The difference in these prices could be significant.

When a call is exercised and you do not own 100 shares of the underlying stock, you are required to deliver those 100 shares at the striking price. This means you have to buy the shares at current market value, no matter how high that price. Because upward price movement, in theory at least, is unlimited, your risk in selling the call is unlimited as well.

Example

Unacceptable Risks: You sell a call for 5 with a striking price of 45 and expiration month of April. At the time, the underlying stock has a market value of $44 per share. You do not own 100 shares of the underlying stock. The day after your order is placed, your brokerage firm deposits $500 into your account (less fees). However, before expiration, the underlying stock's market price soars to $71 per share and your call is exercised. You will lose $2,100—the current market value of 100 shares, $7,100; less the striking price value, $4,500; less the $500 premium you received at the time you sold the call:

Current market value, 100 shares	$7,100
Less striking price	−4,500
Less call premium	−500
Net loss	$2,100

Key Point

Selling uncovered calls is a high-risk strategy, because in theory, a stock's price could rise indefinitely. Every point rise in the stock above striking price is $100 more out of the call seller's pocket.

The risks of selling calls in this manner are extreme. With that in mind, a brokerage firm will allow you to sell calls only if you meet specific requirements. These include having enough equity in your portfolio to provide protection in the event of an unusually high loss. The brokerage firm will want to be able to sell other securities in your account to pay for losses if you cannot come up with the cash. You will need approval in advance from your brokerage firm before you will be allowed to sell calls. Each firm is required to ensure that you understand the risks involved, that you fully understand the options market, and that you have adequate equity and income to undertake those risks.

You will not be allowed to write an unlimited number of naked calls. The potential losses, both to you and to the brokerage firm, place natural limits on this activity. Everyone who wants to sell calls is required to sign a document acknowledging the risks and stating that they understand those risks. In part, this statement includes the following:

Special Statement for Uncovered Option Writers[1]

There are special risks associated with uncovered option writing that expose the investor to potentially significant loss. Therefore, this type of strategy may not be suitable for all customers approved for options transactions.

- The potential loss of uncovered call writing is unlimited. The writer of an uncovered call is in an extremely risky position, and may incur large losses if the value of the underlying instrument increases above the exercise price.

- As with writing uncovered calls, the risk of writing uncovered put options is substantial. The writer of an uncovered put option bears a risk of loss if the value of the underlying instrument declines below the exercise price. Such loss could be substantial if there is a significant decline in the value of the underlying instrument.

- Uncovered option writing is thus suitable only for the knowledgeable investor who understands the risks, has the financial capacity and willingness to incur potentially substantial losses, and has sufficient liquid assets to meet applicable margin requirements. In this regard, if the value of the underlying instrument moves against an uncovered writer's options position, the investor's broker may request significant additional margin payments. If an investor does not make such margin payments, the broker may liquidate stock or options positions in the investor's account, with little or no prior notice in accordance with the investor's margin agreement.

---

[1]From the Options Clearing Corporation, "Risk Disclosure Statement and Acknowledgments," at www.optionsclearing.com.

The requirement that your portfolio include stocks, cash, and other securities in order to sell calls is one form of *margin* requirement imposed by your broker. Such requirements apply not only to option transactions, but also to short selling of stock or, more commonly, to the purchase of securities using funds borrowed from the brokerage firm.

When you enter into an opening sale transaction, you are referred to as a *writer*. Call writers (sellers) hope that the value of the underlying stock will remain at or below the striking price of the call. If that occurs, then the call will expire worthless and the writer's profits will be made from declining time value (as well as any decline in intrinsic value resulting from the stock's price moving from above the striking price, down to or below the striking price). For the writer, the breakeven price is the striking price plus the number of points received for selling the call.

margin

An account with a brokerage firm containing a minimum level of cash and securities to provide collateral for short positions or for purchases for which payment has not yet been made.

Example

Gains Offsetting Losses: You sell a call for 5 with a striking price of 40. Your breakeven is $45 per share (before considering trading costs). Upon exercise, you would be required to deliver 100 shares at the striking price of 40; as long as the stock's current market value is at $45 per share or below, you will not have a loss, even upon exercise, since you received $500 in premium when you sold the call.

It is possible to write a call and make a profit upon exercise. Given the preceding example, if the call were exercised when the stock's market price was $42, you would gain $300 before trading costs:

Current market value, 100 shares	$4,200
Less striking price	−4,000
Loss on the stock	−$200
Option premium received	$500
Profit before trading costs	$300

Key Point

Exercise does not necessarily mean you lose. The call premium discounts a minimal loss because it is yours to keep, even after exercise.

As a writer, you do not have to wait out expiration; you have another choice. You can close out your short position at any time by purchasing the call. You open the position with a sale and close it with a purchase. There are four events that could cause you to close out a short position in your call:

1. The stock's value falls. As a result, time value and intrinsic value, if any, fall as well. The call's premium value is lower, so it is possible to close the position at a profit.

2. The stock's value remains unchanged, but the option's premium value falls due to loss of time value. The call's premium value falls and the position can be closed through purchase, at a profit.

3. The option's premium value remains unchanged because the underlying stock's market value rises. Declining time value is replaced with intrinsic value. The position can be closed at no profit or loss, to avoid exercise.

4. The underlying stock's market value rises enough so that exercise is likely. The position can be closed at a loss to avoid exercise, potentially at greater levels of loss.

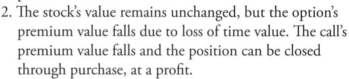

Example

Taking Profits to Escape Risk: You sold a call two months ago for 3. The underlying stock's market value has remained below the striking price without much price movement. Time value has fallen and the option is now worth 1. You have a choice: You can buy the call and close the position, taking a profit of $200; or you can wait for expiration, hoping to keep the entire premium as a profit. This choice exposes you to risk between the decision point and expiration; in the event the stock's market price moves above striking price, intrinsic value could wipe out the profit and lead to exercise. Purchasing to close when the profit is available ensures that profit and enables you to avoid further exposure to risk. If the stock does rise, your breakeven price is 3 points higher than striking price, since you were paid 3 for selling the call.

Whenever you sell a call and you do not also own 100 shares of stock, your risk is described as a *naked position*, which refers to the continuous exposure to risk from the moment of sale through to expiration. Remember, the buyer can exercise at any time, and exercise can happen at any time that your naked call is in the money. Even though exercise is most likely at the time just before expiration, there is no guarantee that it will not happen before that time.

Example

Going Naked, More than Merely Embarrassing:
You sold a naked call last week that had four months to go until expiration. You were not worried about exercise. However, as of today, the stock has risen above the striking price and your call is in the money. Your brokerage firm has advised that your call was exercised. You are required to deliver 100 shares of the underlying stock at the striking price. Your call no longer exists.

In this example, you experience a loss on the stock because you are required to purchase 100 shares at current market value and deliver them at the striking price. Even so, you may have an overall profit if the gap between current market value and striking price is less than the amount you received when you sold the call.

liquid market

A market in which buyers and sellers are matched to one another, and the exchange absorbs any imbalances between the two sides.

You can never predict early exercise, since buyer and seller are not matched one-to-one. The selection is random. The Options Clearing Corporation (OCC) acts as buyer to every seller, and as seller to every buyer. This ensures a *liquid market* even when one side of the transaction is much larger than the other. When a buyer decides to exercise a call, the order is assigned at random to a seller, or on the basis of first-in, first-out. You will not know that this has happened to you until your broker gets in touch to inform you of the exercise. In-the-money options are automatically exercised by the OCC on exercise date.

Key Point

Because exercise can happen at any time your call is in the money, you need to be aware of your exposure; early exercise is always a possibility. If you sell an in-the-money call, exercise could happen quickly, even on the same day.

In order to profit from selling calls, you will need the underlying stock to act in one of two ways:

1. Its market value must remain at or below the striking price of the call, waiting out the evaporation of time value. The option will expire worthless, or it can be closed with a purchase amount lower than the initial sales price.
2. The market value must remain at a stable enough price that the option can be purchased below initial sales price, even if it is in the money. The decline in time value still occurs, even when accompanied by consistent levels of intrinsic value.

The profit and loss zones for uncovered calls are summarized in Figure 5.1. Because you receive cash for selling a call, the breakeven price is higher than the striking price. In this illustration, a call was sold for 5; hence, breakeven is five points higher than striking price. (This example does not take into account the transaction fees.) To enter into a naked call position, you will need to work with your brokerage firm to meet its requirements.

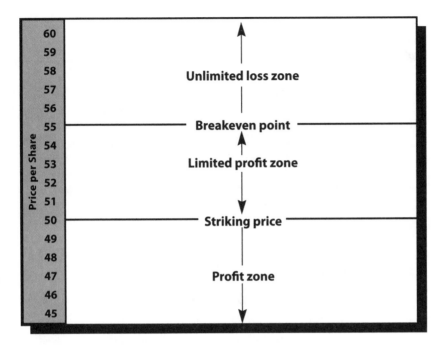

Figure 5.1 An Uncovered Call's Profit and Loss Zones

Example

Setting Limits: You have advised your broker that you intend to write uncovered calls. Your portfolio currently is valued at $20,000 in securities and cash. Your broker restricts your uncovered call writing activity to a level that, in the broker's estimation, would not potentially exceed $20,000. However, as market conditions change, your portfolio value could fall, in which case your broker has the right to restrict your uncovered call activity to a lower dollar amount, or even to require you to deposit additional funds. When you do not have funds available, the brokerage firm has the right to sell some of your securities to cover the shortfall.

Potential loss in call writing is conceivably unlimited because no one knows how high a stock's price could rise. Put writers, in comparison, face a limited form of potential loss. The maximum is the difference between the striking price and zero; in practical terms, the real risk level is the difference between the striking price and tangible book value per share.

Example

Worst Case, but Limited: You want to write puts in your portfolio as part of your investment strategy (see Chapter 6). Your portfolio is valued at $20,000. Your brokerage firm will place restrictions on uncovered put writing activity based on an estimation of potential losses. However, when you write puts, your liability is not as great; stocks can fall only so far, whereas they can rise indefinitely. So the worst case for selling puts is known; it is the striking price of the short puts.

Assessing Uncovered Call Writing Risks

Don't forget the importance of risk assessment in determining what is an appropriate investment or strategy. Consider the risks involved with writing uncovered calls, especially in light of limitations that are placed on your activity by brokerage firms. These limitations are necessary due to the risk of potential losses. Restrictions that are placed on naked call writing limit your ability to participate in the high-risk end of this market.

The risks of uncovered call writing include the following:

- The stock might rise in value; you will be required to buy the call to close your position and avoid further loss.
- The stock might rise in value, leading to exercise, perhaps early exercise.
- Although the stock might remain at or below striking price for a period of time, it could rise unexpectedly and suddenly, leading to exercise; you are at risk from the moment you sell the call, all the way to expiration.
- You lose opportunities to move your capital around in the market because your brokerage firm wants to limit your risk of loss as well as theirs; so your equity is committed as collateral for your open uncovered call positions.
- If you do suffer unexpected large losses, your brokerage firm may sell other securities in your portfolio to pay for those losses. This

may include securities whose sale is poorly timed, so you lose long-term value in your portfolio, not to mention control over the timing of a stock's sale.

- Although you set standards for yourself, you might fail to take action when you should, so that today's profit disappears and you end up losing money upon exercise or having to buy the call at a loss to avoid exercise.

Key Point

It is smart to know all the risks involved with uncovered call selling. Not knowing can lead to some very expensive surprises.

A Question of Suitability

Are uncovered calls suitable for you? Every investor and trader has to ask this question at the very beginning of consideration for any strategy. Uncovered calls are extremely risky because, in theory at least, a stock's market value can rise indefinitely. As a practical matter, a stock's potential price increase is limited, but it is impossible to know by how much; and that is where the risk factor is so extreme.

The level of suitability is determined by several crucial factors. These include:

- Risk level and your ability to accept it. The most important test for any strategy is whether the risk level is appropriate. Can you afford the "worst-case" outcome? In the example of a covered call, the maximum risk is unknown, and it could be substantial. For example, what happens if you sell an uncovered call with a striking price of 50 and receive a premium of 6 ($600)? Without considering transaction fees, you would break even if the call were exercised when the stock's market value had risen to $56 per share. But what if the stock rises to $66. Or $76?

Some options traders are willing to undertake the risk involved with uncovered calls. Because three-quarters of all options expire worthless, the law of averages mandates that in a majority of instances, short options will not be exercised. But a string of modest profits can be easily wiped out by one unexpected rise in a stock's market price.

- Knowledge about the strategy and risk. No one should ever enter into a strategy without fully understanding the risks involved. Many first-time options traders become excited by the potential for profits, but ignore the equally important potential for loss. So a strategy like writing uncovered calls can be lucrative but also high risk.

Every brokerage firm is required to determine whether a customer has adequate knowledge to trade options. Before you are allowed to do any options trading, you will be asked to complete an options application and state your level of experience. But this requirement is only one aspect of the requirement for knowledge, and it is a requirement intended not only to protect you but also to protect your brokerage firm. Equally important is the more

practical requirement that your actual experience match the strategies. You can easily claim to have extensive knowledge when you fill out a form, but you might not be fully aware of the actual risks you face when writing uncovered calls or undertaking other high-risk strategies.

- *Experience as an investor or trader.* Knowing the risks of an options strategy is all-important, but so is experience. Having a book-smarts understanding of uncovered calls is a good start, but you also need actual experience. For example, the knowledge that three-quarters of all options expire worthless might compel you to make a logical assumption: that uncovered call risks are not all that high. Since time value evaporates over time, selling calls with high time value reduces risks, as the logical argument goes. However, once you actually enter into a short option position, you are likely to discover that the strategy is not nearly as comfortable as you had thought.

  Actual, real-money experience is an essential requirement for options trading. There is no substitute for it. The syndrome of theoretical experience versus real-world experience has misled many people. For example, in recent years, online gambling has become widespread. Anyone who has practiced card games online with artificial pots of money knows that the strategic play level is not the same as the play level with actual money. You might believe you are an exceptionally lucky card player. But when you put real dollars on the table, a man named Doc might quickly clean you out.

  The same caution applies to options trading. Some strategies are highly conservative (as you will see in the next section of this chapter). Other strategies, specifically writing uncovered calls, are extremely high risk and not appropriate for everyone. Your experience as a stock investor and options trader is invaluable in knowing quite well what levels of risk you can afford to take and what levels you are willing to take.

- *Income and investment capital.* You need to have enough money in your portfolio to afford writing uncovered calls. Even if you believe you can manage the risk to this strategy, you cannot write an unlimited number of short calls. Your brokerage firm has to limit your exposure by law.

  The Federal Reserve Board (FRB) has a hand in regulating how much risk you can have outstanding in your brokerage account. The FRB enforces *Regulation T,* which defines the level of credit you can have in your brokerage account. Reg T limits your borrowing power to 50 percent of the purchase price of securities. So when you write an uncovered call, your brokerage firm has to limit your risk by requiring that you keep the required cash level in your account.

Uncovered calls have a very specific margin requirement. When you write an uncovered call, you are required to maintain at least 20 percent of the stock's current price plus the amount of the call premium, and minus the dollar value that the stock is below the striking price. You are always required to maintain at least 10 percent of the stock's price even when this computation ends up with an amount below that level. Examples are summarized in the following:

Call Written	Current Stock Price	Call Price	20% of Price	Difference	Margin Required
60	$65	$600	$1,100	$0	$1,700
50	50	300	1,000	0	1,300
40	37	200	800	300	700
30	$21	$200	$600	$900	$210*

*The margin cannot be less than 10 percent of the stock price.

In the summary, the calculation is performed based on four different uncovered call scenarios. In the first two cases, the stock price is higher than striking price or equal to it, so no in-the-money difference applies. In the last case, the calculation is performed in the same way as in the other cases (call price plus 20 percent of stock value, minus in-the-money difference), but it produces a negative. The minimum required is 10 percent of the current stock price ($21 per share × 10% = $210).

• *Personal investment goals.* If you want to preserve your capital and take low risks, uncovered call writing is clearly inappropriate for you. Everyone has a set of personal investment goals, and it is not always a clear-cut issue of a strategy's being 100 percent appropriate or inappropriate. This is why some self-analysis is useful before putting money at risk. If you are a speculator and you want only high-risk and high-return strategies, then uncovered call writing is a great concept. But if you are saving for retirement, a child's college education, or to purchase your first home, uncovered call writing would be reckless. The approach calling for higher risk as a means for making profits more rapidly is often ill advised. If you cannot

afford to lose money, you should not enter into strategies in which losses are very real possibilities.

- *Brokerage approval level.* Finally, your brokerage firm is going to assign you *an approval level* based on your experience as an options trader. These levels vary slightly among brokerage firms, but generally they follow the same restrictions.

    For example, at level 0, customers are approved for the most conservative of strategies, such as writing covered calls. Level 1 allows customers to buy calls and puts and to enter other long-side advanced strategies in addition to all trading allowed under level 0. (Long-side means you cannot open uncovered short positions.) At level 2, customers can enter all strategies in level 1 plus more complex strategies known as spreads (more on this later in the book). Level 3 is the highest level, allowing customers to enter virtually every kind of option strategy and limited only by margin and brokerage restrictions. These include uncovered options and advanced strategies.

Your personal suitability is not limited to knowledge and experience. Brokerage firms assign levels based on capital available in your account, in addition to your skill level. For example, if the total value of your account is only $5,000, it is unlikely that you will get the highest approval level.

Risk and suitability are much different when you sell covered calls, as the next section explains.

SELLING COVERED CALLS

When you sell uncovered calls, potentially large losses can result if you are required to deliver shares upon exercise, or to close out positions at a loss to avoid exercise. Imagine being able to sell calls without that risk— meaning that you would never be required to suffer large losses due to an unexpected rise in the stock's market value.

There is a way. By selling a call when you also own 100 shares of the underlying stock, you *cover* your position. If the option is called away by the buyer, you can meet the obligation simply by delivering shares that you already own.

You enjoy several advantages through the *covered call*.

- You are paid a premium for each call that you sell, and the cash is placed in your account at the time you sell. While this is also true of uncovered call writing, the same risks do not apply. You can afford exercise because you own 100 shares of stock. Upon exercise, you would not be required to buy shares at market price; you simply relinquish ownership of the shares you already own.

- The actual net price of your 100 shares of stock is reduced by the value of the option premium. The covered call discounts your basis because you receive cash when you sell the call. This gives you flexibility and downside protection, as well as greater versatility in selling calls with high time value.

Examples

A Premium Deal: You owned 100 shares of Merck that you had originally bought at $38 per share. You sold a covered call shortly after buying the stock at 40 and were paid 3 ($300). However, when the stock rose to $42 per share shortly before expiration, your covered call was exercised. Your stock was called away at the striking price of $40 per share. During the period you owned the stock, you received four quarterly dividends at $38 each. Your total profit on this transaction was:

Profit on stock ($40 less original cost of $38)	$200
Call premium received	300
Dividends received	152
Total	$652

Discounted Basis: You owned 100 shares of Merck you had originally bought at $38 per share, as in the previous example. You waited a few months until the stock's market value had risen to $42 per share. At that time you sold a covered call with a striking price of 45 and received a premium of 2 ($200). Your net basis is reduced to $36 per share (original cost less premium on the option). While you continue to face the possibility of exercise at $45, that would be 9 points higher than your net basis in the stock.

- Selling covered calls provides you with the freedom to accept modern interim price declines, because the premium you receive reduces your basis in the stock. Simply owning the stock without the discount means that declines in the stock's market value represent paper losses.

Example

Riding the Price Waves: You own stock originally purchased at $38 per share. Since the purchase date, the price has moved between $38 and $44 per share. When the price was on the high side, you sold covered calls, closing out those positions when the stock's price retreated. You have made a series of modest but consistent profits on the movement in the stock, without having to take profits. The sum of your profits has also reduced your net basis in the stock.

- By selling calls against appreciated stock, you are able to augment profits and, in the case of exercise, build in a capital gain as well.

Example

Tax and Profit Planning: You employ a strategy of buying stock and waiting for price appreciation, and then selling covered calls. If the calls are exercised, you achieve a capital gain on the stock as well as dividend income and option premium. If the calls are not exercised, you augment your current income by closing out those calls at a lower price, or waiting until expiration.

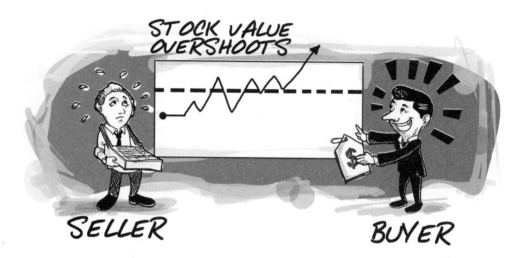

The disadvantage to covered call selling is found in lost opportunity risk that may or may not materialize. If the stock's market value rises dramatically, your call will be exercised at the specified striking price. If you had not sold the call, you would benefit from higher market value in shares of stock. So covered call sellers trade the certainty of premiums received today, for the potential lost profits in the event of exercise.

Key Point

The major risk associated with covered call writing is the possibility of lost income from rising stock prices. But that might not happen at all; when you sell a call, you accept the possibility of lost capital gains income in exchange for the certainty of call premium income.

Example

Profit Alternatives, a Nice Dilemma: You own 100 shares of stock, which you bought last year at $50 per share. Current market value is $54 per share. You are willing to sell this stock at a profit. You write a November 55 call and receive a premium of 5. Now your net basis in the stock is $45 per share (original price of $50 per share, discounted 5 points by the option premium). If the stock's market value remains between the range of $45 and $55 between the date you sell the call and expiration, the short call will expire worthless. It would not be exercised within that price range, since striking price is 55. You can wait out expiration or buy the call, closing it out at a profit. However, if the stock's value does rise above $55 per share and the call is exercised, you would not receive any gain above $55 per share. While exercise would still produce a profit of $1,000 ($500 stock profit plus $500 option premium), you would lose any profits above the striking price level.

One of three events can take place when you sell a covered call: an increase in the stock's price, a decrease in the stock's price, or no significant change. As long as you own 100 shares of the underlying stock, you continue to receive dividends even when you have sold the call. The value of writing calls should be compared to the value of buying and holding stock, as shown in Table 5.1.

Table 5.1 Comparing Strategies

	Outcomes	
Event	**Owning Stock and Writing Calls**	**Owning Stock Only**
Stock goes up in value.	Call is exercised; profits are limited to striking price and call premium.	Stock can be sold at a profit.
Stock remains at or below the striking price.	Time value declines; the call can be closed out at a profit or allowed to expire worthless.	No profit or loss until sold.
Stock declines in value.	Stock price is discounted by call premium; the call is closed or allowed to expire worthless.	Loss on the stock.
Dividends	Earned while stock is held.	Earned while stock is held.

Before you undertake any strategy, assess the benefits or consequences in the event of all possible outcomes, including the potential for lost future profits that might or might not occur in the stock. To ensure a profit in the outcome of writing covered calls, it is wise to select those calls with striking prices above your original basis, or above original basis when discounted by the call premium you receive.

Example

The Discounting Effect: You bought stock last year at $48 per share. If you sell a covered call with a striking price of 50 and receive a premium of 3, you have discounted your basis to $45 per share. Given the same original basis, you may be able to sell a call with a striking price of 45 and receive a premium of 8. That discounts your basis to $40 per share; in both instances, exercise would net a profit of $500. (Exercise at $50, discounted basis of $45 per share; or exercise at $45, discounted basis of $40 per share.) In the latter case, chances of exercise are greater because the call is 5 points deeper in the money. Selling out-of-the-money calls also affects your capital gain, so if your profit in the stock is substantial, this strategy could be expensive; if you lose the long-term gain status in the stock, it could offset the overall pretax gain.

lock in

To freeze the price of the underlying stock by selling a covered call. As long as the call position is open, the writer is locked into the striking price, regardless of current market value of the stock. In the event of exercise, the stock is delivered at the locked-in price.

In comparing potential profits from various strategies, you might conclude that writing in-the-money calls makes sense in some circumstances, even with possible tax consequences in mind. A decline in the stock's price reduces call premium dollar-for-dollar, with the added advantage of declining time value. If this occurs, you can close out the position at a profit, or simply wait for exercise. As a call seller, you are willing to *lock in* the price of the underlying stock in the event of exercise; this makes sense only if exercise will produce a profit to you, given original purchase price of the shares, discounted by the call premium, and given the net tax consequences involved.

Example

Lock In: To freeze the price of the underlying stock by selling a covered call. As long as the call position is open, the writer is locked into the striking price, regardless of current market value of the stock. In the event of exercise, the stock is delivered at the locked-in price.

Assessing Covered Call Writing Risks

The seller of uncovered calls faces potentially large losses. As a covered call writer, your risks are reduced significantly. That risk is limited on the upside to lost future profits that do not always take place. On the downside, the risk is the same for simply owning shares; a decline in price represents a paper loss. The call writer discounts the basis in stock, providing a degree of downside protection and lowering those risks. When you write calls against stock using striking prices above your original basis, you have created a built-in profit factor. Whereas uncovered call selling is very high-risk, covered call writing is on the opposite side of the spectrum; it is very low-risk.

Key Point

The covered call seller has fewer risks than others because it is a safe, conservative strategy. Even if the stock falls in value, writing calls provides you with downside protection.

You may be concerned with the lost opportunity risk associated with potential future profits in the stock. Once you sell a call, you commit yourself to selling 100 shares at the striking price, even if the stock's market value rises far above that price. Owning 100 shares covers the short position in the call; it also limits potential profit overall if the call is exercised. Profits are not limited as a certainty; if you close the position or roll into a different short position, or if the call expires worthless, then the lost profit risk is eliminated.

By properly structuring a covered call writing strategy, you can learn to manage the risk of losing potential future gains, in exchange for predictability and the certainty of current profits. The covered call writing strategy is going to produce profits consistently when applied correctly. So, a very good return on your investment—including double-digit returns—is possible through writing covered calls. You might lose the occasional spectacular profit when a stock's price rises suddenly; but for the most part, your rate of return will exceed what you could expect in your portfolio without writing covered calls. Some pitfalls to avoid in your covered call writing strategy are:

- *Setting up the call write so that, if exercised, you end up losing money in the underlying stock.* This is possible if you sell calls with striking prices below your original basis in the stock.

- *Getting locked into positions that you cannot afford to close out.* If you become involved in a high level of covered call writing, you may eventually find yourself in a position where you want to close out the calls, but you do not have the cash available to take advantage of the situation. You need to set up an adequate cash reserve so that you can act when the opportunity is there.

- *Writing calls on the wrong stock.* When you begin comparing premium values, you might spot an unusually rich time value in a particular option. The stock is likely to be volatile, which is the cause of the exceptionally high premium in the call; this means that the risks associated with owning that stock are greater than for less volatile issues.

CALCULATING RATE OF RETURN

If your purpose in owning stock is to hold it for many years, writing calls may not be an appropriate strategy—although, in some instances, this strategy can be used to enhance returns with only a moderate risk of exercise. But the call writer's objective often is quite different from that of the long-term investor and, while the two objectives can coexist, it is more likely that you will use the covered call writing strategy on a portion of your portfolio, while avoiding even moderate risks of exercise on another portion. You have three potential sources of income as a covered call writer:

1. Call premium
2. Capital gain on stock
3. Dividends

This example shows how a potential future profit may be lost, a fact that covered call writers need to accept. Simply owning stock and not writing calls against it could produce profits in the event of a large run-up in price, but it also produces losses in the event of price decline, and selling calls provides downside protection in addition to the certainty of profit.

We have to deal with averages in order to compare straight stock ownership to covered call writing. If we simply hold shares of stock, some will soar in value and others will perform dismally. On average, we may expect to realize a return that beats inflation. For example, the compound rate of return for the S&P 500 from 1926 to 1997 was 12.4 percent. During the same period, the Consumer Price Index averaged 3.1 percent, so stock investments (measured by the S&P 500) beat inflation.[1] If we accept the premise that a portfolio is likely to perform on average at that rate, can we do better by utilizing stocks through covered call writing? Remember, the exceptional stock could return triple digits due to unexpected price growth, and, equally likely, exceptions will involve price declines or stagnation. On average, a compound rate of return should be about 12.4 percent. If we select stocks wisely and employ smart covered call strategies, can we enhance this rate of return? Even given the exceptions on both upside and downside, covered call writing does improve overall returns on portfolios, often dramatically.

[1]Bureau of Labor Statistics, at www.bls.gov/cpi

Example

Double-Digit Returns: You bought 100 shares of stock and paid $32 per share. Several months later, the stock's market value rose to $38 per share. You wrote a March 35 call and received 8. Your reasoning: Your original basis in the stock was $32, and selling the call discounts that basis to $24. If the call were exercised, you would be required to deliver the shares at $35, regardless of current market value of those shares. Your profit would be $1,100 if that occurred, a return of 34.4 percent. The option premium at the time you sold contained 3 points of intrinsic value and 5 points of time value. If the stock's market value remained at the same level without exercise, that 5 points eventually would evaporate and the call could be closed through purchase at a lower premium. If the stock's market value were to rise far above the striking price, you would still be required to deliver shares at the striking price upon exercise; the potential future gain would be lost. By undertaking this strategy, you exchange the certainty of a 34.4 percent gain for the uncertainty of greater profits later, if they materialize.

A realistic point of view may be to count profits only if they are taken. In other words, potential future profits do not exist at the time to sell an option, and by the same argument, profits in open option positions are not profits unless you close those positions. Covered call writers can earn consistent returns on their strategies, but they also have to accept the occasional lost profit from a stock's unexpected price change. Because covered call writing provides downside protection and discounts your basis in the stock, the strategy also reduces the potential for losses due to short-term price decline.

Key Point

When considering the risk of losing future profits that may or may not materialize, it makes sense to also evaluate the potential for future losses from owning stock, and to consider how selling covered calls mitigates that risk.

By accepting the limitation associated with writing covered calls, you trade off the potential gain for the *discount* in the price of the stock. This downside protection is especially desirable when you remember that you also continue to receive dividends even though you have sold calls.

You also need to study profit and loss zones applicable in every strategy, and one example is shown in Figure 5.2. A covered call's profit and loss zones are determined by the combination of two factors: option premium value and the underlying stock's current market value. If the stock falls below the breakeven price (price paid for the stock, minus the premium received for selling the call) there will be a loss. Of course, as a stockholder, you decide when and if to sell, so the loss is not necessarily realized. You have the luxury of being able to let the option expire worthless, and then wait for a rebound in the stock's price. The option premium discounts your basis, so by selling the call, you lower the required rebound level.

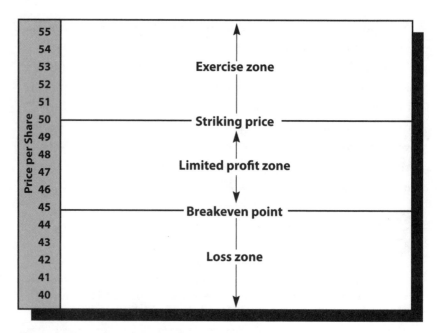

Figure 5.2 A Covered Call's Profit and Loss Zones

You also need to calculate the rate of return that will be realized given different outcomes. Apply one critical rule for yourself: Never sell a covered call unless you would be satisfied with the outcome in the event of exercise. Figure the *total return* before selling the call, and enter into the transaction only when you are confident that the numbers work for you.

Total return in the case of exercise includes appreciation of stock market value, call premium, and dividend income. If the option expires worthless, one rate of return results; if you close the option by buying it before expiration, a different return results. Because the second outcome does not include selling the stock, the rate of return can vary considerably. The return is calculated based on the original purchase of the stock. The fact that a different base applies for the different calculations makes a yield comparison elusive. So the relative return calculations should not be used to compare outcomes, but to evaluate your overall risk in entering into a particular covered call strategy. The acceptable strategy is one in which you would be happy with the rate of return in any of the outcome scenarios.

Example

A Table of the Elements: You own 100 shares of stock that you bought at $41 per share. Current market value is $44 per share, and you have sold a July 45 call for 5. Between now and expiration, you will receive a total of $40 in dividend income.

6 SELLING PUTS: THE OVERLOOKED STRATEGY

The place where optimism most flourishes is the lunatic asylum.
—Havelock Ellis, *The Dance of Life*, 1923

Selling puts is an optimistic strategy. You will profit if and when the stock's market value rises; even so, it is easy to forget this because so much emphasis is placed on calls. The incredible feature of options trading is that strategies can be devised to suit any type of market and any level of risk. Evaluate puts for their potential, and compare short put risks to the risk of long calls. Their profile is identical; the risks are far different.

Comparing short puts to long calls is only one of the comparisons worth making. You may be well aware of the special risks involved in selling calls and may consider short puts to fit into the same risk category; this is a mistake. When you sell uncovered calls, a number of things can occur: The underlying stock could rise indefinitely, so that, in theory, risk is unlimited. Even when you write covered calls, you still face the risk of lost future profits because striking prices lock in the option seller to a fixed price in the event of exercise.

The situation is completely different when you sell puts. The put is the opposite of a call, so as a put seller, you hope that the value of the underlying stock will rise. As the stock rises, the value of the put falls, creating a profit. You also face the risk that the stock's market value will fall. In that case, you experience a loss; however, this loss is finite. The greatest loss possible, in theory, is zero, but a stock is unlikely to fall that far. A well-selected company's stock will have a limited likely range of market price; for example, while market value could fall below a company's tangible book value per share, it does not stand to reason that market price would decline far below that level.

Key Point

Selling calls cannot be compared to selling covered calls. Short puts are always uncovered. However, risk is quite limited compared to uncovered calls because stock can decline only so far.

Even a drastic decline in a stock's market value has limited consequences for the put seller. The risk of loss is confined, realistically, to the price range between striking price and book value; that is the lowest reasonable price level. There is no guarantee, however, and the market has shown time and again that price levels are relatively oblivious to the intrinsic value of stock. In other words, the fundamentals serve as a valuable means for evaluating a company's long-term growth potential, but short-term price changes are unreliable; the fundamentals mean little in terms of pricing over the next few months. Short-term indicators are unstable for any purpose of analysis. The market can be viewed as having reliable intermediate and long-term trends showing up through indicators; but the short-term trends are highly chaotic and unreliable, and this is where option risks reside.

Tangible book value per share—book value minus all intangible assets such as goodwill—is a fundamental *support level* for the valuation of stock. It is today's financial worth, without considering any prospects for future growth. A popular investing concept, *value investing*, means just that. You will do better buying a company's value, not a stock's price. So when analysts publish a target range for a stock, it makes sense to question (1) how the target range was arrived at, (2) whether price targeting is based on fundamentals, and (3) how price equates to the company's long-term investment value.

tangible book value per share

The net value of a company, computed by subtracting all liabilities from all assets, and further reducing the net by all intangible assets. The net of tangible assets is then divided by the number of outstanding shares of common stock.

Valuable Resource
Tangible book value per share is not difficult to calculate. It is simply the total net worth of a company minus its intangible assets. To see more, link to **www.ehow.com/how_4694957_stock-using-tangible-book-value.html**.

Example

A Finite Risk Strategy: You bought 100 shares of Yahoo (YHOO) and paid $11 per share. When the stock had risen to $15 per share, you sold a four-month put in the belief that the stock would continue to rise in value. Striking price was 15 and you received a premium of 1.07 ($107). Tangible book value per share at the time was $7.05 per share. Given these facts, your maximum risk was $288:

Purchase price of stock	$1,100
Less: premium received for put	− 107
Net basis in stock	$ 993
Tangible book value	− 705
Net risk	$ 288

value investing

An approach to picking stocks based on actual value of the company rather than on price or price targets.

You sold this put because you believed that $15 per share was a reasonable price; given the premium of $107, the price upon exercise would be reduced to less than $14 per share, nearly a full point below the value of stock on the day you sold the put. This is one of several ways to use options as a form of purchasing additional shares of stock at a discount.

In this example, the "net risk" represents the risk if and when the company were to be completely liquidated. In other words, Yahoo would have to sell all its assets and settle up with its creditors, leaving stockholders with $7.05 per share. A put seller evaluates this as the maximum risk, but, realistically, the exposure is far less. The $107 return on a $1,100 investment (before annualizing) is 9.7 percent. Because the put expires in four months (meaning risk exposure only lasts that long), annualized return should be three times greater, or 29.1 percent.

One additional point concerning tangible book value per share: While it is useful in estimating the true net risk based on book value, assets might be worth considerably more than their tangible, stated value. This is because assets may be worth more than their net book value, especially appreciating capital assets (like real estate) that are depreciated each year but could be gaining in market value.

A put is an option to sell 100 shares of the underlying stock, at a fixed price by a specific date in the future. So when you sell a put, you grant the buyer the right to "put" 100 shares of stock to you at the striking price, to sell you 100 shares. In exchange for receiving a premium at the time of your opening sale transaction, you accept the risk of exercise. You are willing, as a put seller, to buy 100 shares of the underlying stock even though at the time of exercise, current value of the shares will be lower than the fixed striking price.

Key Point

It makes sense to sell puts as long as you believe that the striking price is a fair value for that company's stock.

As a put seller, you reduce your exposure to risk by selecting stocks within a limited price range. For example, if you sell puts with striking prices of 50 or less, your maximum loss is 50 points, or $5,000; that, of course, would occur only if a stock were to become worthless by expiration date. If you sell puts with striking price of 25 or lower, the maximum exposure is cut in half, to $2,500 per contract. However, the more realistic way to assess maximum risk is to identify book value per share in comparison to striking price. That gap represents a more likely range of risk, regardless of the stock's current market value.

ANALYZING STOCK VALUES

If you consider the striking price to be fair and reasonable for 100 shares of the underlying stock, selling puts has two advantages:

1. You receive cash at the point that you sell a put.
2. The premium you receive discounts your basis in the stock in the event of exercise.

If you are willing to purchase shares of stock at the striking price, then selling puts is a smart strategy. You may even argue that there is no actual risk because you believe the stock price is reasonable. If, as an alternative, you were to purchase 100 shares of stock today, you would pay the

current price without receiving a premium for selling a put; and the market value is just as likely to decline as if you were to sell the put.

Buying shares above market value may be acceptable if you plan to keep those shares as a long-term investment, considering (a) the discounting effect from selling puts and (b) the possibility of generating profits from selling puts that are not exercised. If the difference between striking price and current market value at the time of exercise is greater than the amount you received in premium, you have a paper loss at the point of exercise. In that outcome, you will need to wait out the time required for the stock's price to rebound before you can recapture that loss. You may be able to offset this loss by selling covered calls against stock acquired in this manner.

Acquiring stock through writing puts has to be done with the stock's value as the essential element in the decision. Remember, *value* does not mean the current market value of the stock; it means the price you are willing to pay per share. Put sellers, like call sellers, usually prefer to avoid exercise, so they use rolling techniques, such as rolling forward and down, for example, to either defer exercise or reduce the eventual exercise price. Once you identify the degree of risk involved with exercise, you need to compare that to the premium income in order to determine whether placing yourself in a short position is worth that risk exposure. If you embark on a program of put writing, you will need to have available adequate capital to purchase the shares of stock involved, an important factor that limits the degree of put writing you are likely to undertake. In fact, you will be required to have adequate funds on hand in your brokerage account. If you experience a high volume of exercise, you will use up your available capital and fill your portfolio with shares of stock acquired above current market value. So you naturally need to limit put writing to those stocks you would like to own whether you wrote puts or not.

Example

Calculating the Put Advantage: You sold a put with a striking price of 55 and received 6 (discounting the net price per share to $49). You considered $49 per share a reasonable price for those shares. Before expiration, the stock's market value fell to $48 and your put was exercised.

Two observations need to be made concerning this transaction:

1. The outcome is acceptable as long as you believe that $49 per share is a fair price for the stock. You would then also believe that current market value—only 1 point lower than your basis—is likely to rebound in the future. If your assumption is correct, the loss is a paper loss only and it will turn out to be a worthwhile investment.

2. If the stock's market value had risen, you would have profited from selling the put. It would not have been exercised and would have expired worthless; or time value would have evaporated, enabling you to buy to close at a profit. In those outcomes, the put premium would have been all profit. So selling puts in a rising market can produce profits when you are unwilling to tie up capital to buy 100 shares; this can be achieved with limited risk exposure.

Put sellers who seek only the income from premiums need to select stocks that they consider to be good prospects for price increase. Premium value is only half the test of a viable put sale; the other half is careful selection of stocks. As a put seller, you have to be willing to acquire 100 shares of stock for each short put written. If risks are too great, or if you do not want to acquire shares, then you cannot justify the strategy.

EVALUATING RISKS

Comparisons between selling calls and selling puts provide good insights about risk. Stock selection contains specific risks for call sellers. More attractive option premiums are associated with more volatile stocks. So covered call writers may be prone to selecting higher-risk stocks in order to sell higher-than-average time value.

The same risks apply to put sellers. Higher time value premiums for puts are going to be found on stocks with higher-than-average volatility. The direction of price movement you desire is different with puts than with calls, but the risks in the underlying stock are the same. Put sellers face the risk that the underlying stock's market value will fall. The more drastically the price falls, the greater the risk of exercise. However, a put seller's perception of risk has to be different from that of the call seller. The key to selecting puts should not be the size of the premium, but your willingness to buy the stock at the striking price in the event of exercise. Depending solely on premium dollar value can be deceiving as well. For example, a put premium of 4 on a $30 stock with a striking price of 30 provides 4 points of downside protection and, in the event of exercise, a return of 13.3 percent. A premium of 8—twice as much—on a $90 stock with a striking price of 90 represents a return if the put is exercised of 8.9 percent. Exercise in the first example would require you to purchase stock at $30, and in the second example you would be required to invest $90 per share. So your exercise cost would be three times higher ($9,000 versus $3,000) but your if-exercised rate of return would be about two-thirds as good. This demonstrates that depending solely on premium levels can be very deceiving. A more realistic evaluation of risk is required to make a logical decision.

However, selling puts does require planning and risk evaluation in the same manner as selling calls. For example, the *margin requirement* a brokerage firm imposes as a hard-and-fast rule means you have to plan ahead and have equity on hand before you begin selling puts. This naturally limits the transaction volume, since no one has unlimited equity in his or her portfolio.

margin requirement

The maximum amount of outstanding risk investors are allowed to hold in their portfolio, or the maximum unfunded dollar level allowed when trading on margin.

Key Point

Whenever you sell puts, your brokerage firm is going to require that you have at least 50 percent of the exercise price left on deposit. In this way, in the case of exercise, your margin requirement will be met.

PUT STRATEGIES

There are five popular strategies for selling puts: to produce short-term income, to make use of idle cash deposits in a brokerage account, to buy stocks, to cover short stock positions, or to create a tax put.

Strategy 1: Producing Income

The most popular reason for selling puts is also the most apparent: the purely speculative idea of earning short-term profits from put premiums. The ideal outcome would be a decline in put value from falling time and intrinsic value, enabling you to purchase and close the short position at a profit. Time is on your side when you sell, so the more time value in the total premium, the better your chances for profit.

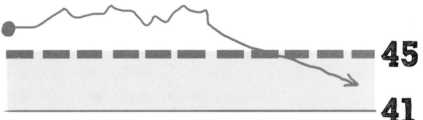

STRIKING PRICE 45

45

41

LIMITED OR BREAK EVEN PROFIT

Example

The Put Time Strategy: Last January, you sold a June 45 put for 4. At that time, the underlying stock's market value was $46 per share. Because market value was higher than the striking price, the entire premium was time value. (For puts, in-the-money is opposite than for calls.) If the stock's market value remained at or above $45 per share, the put would eventually expire worthless. If by exercise date stock is valued between $41 and $45 per share, you would earn a limited profit or break even in the event of exercise (before trading costs). The $41 per share level is 4 points below striking price, and you received $400 for selling the put.

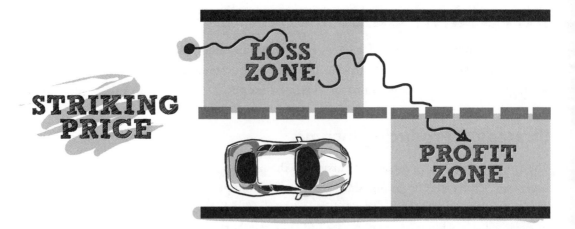

A short position can be canceled at any time. As a seller, you can close the position by buying the put at the current premium level. However, the buyer has the right to exercise the put at any time. So when you sell a put, you are exposed to exercise if that put is in the money (when the stock's market value is lower than striking price). For the premium you receive, you willingly expose yourself to this risk.

You can make an informed decision about short puts by being aware of the profit and loss zones in any open positions. From this analysis, you are able to decide in advance at what point to close the positions or how long to keep them open. This self-imposed goal is related to premium level, the status of current market value in relation to striking price, and the degree of time value premium remaining. If a profit becomes unlikely or impossible, you have the choice of closing the position and accepting a limited loss.

 Key Point

Options traders recognize that they cannot be right all the time. It often is wisest to accept a small loss rather than continue to be exposed to potentially greater losses.

An example of profit and loss zones for selling a put is shown in Figure 6.1. This is based on a striking price of 50 with a put premium of 6. The premium creates a 6-point limited profit zone between $44 and $50 per share and a profit zone above striking price. Below the breakeven point of $44, you will experience a loss. This visual range analysis helps you to define when and where you will close a position, based on proximity between a stock's current market value and loss zone.

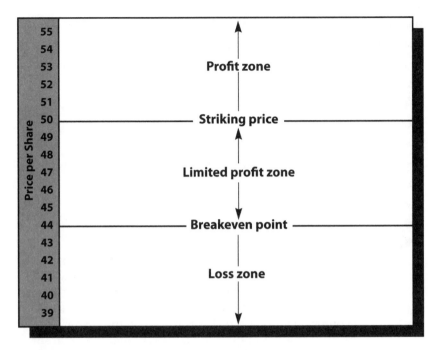

Figure 6.1 Put Selling Profit and Loss Zones

It is possible to close the put at a profit even when the stock's market value falls below striking price. This relies on time value decline. The analysis of profit and loss zones in Figure 6.1 is based on the worst-case assumption about where a stock's price will end up at the point of expiration. If the premium contains a good amount of time value, you can profit merely by trading in the put, even when considerable price movement occurs. Of course, whenever it moves to an in-the-money range, you also risk exercise.

Conceivably, you could select stocks that will remain at or above the striking price and earn premium profits repeatedly, without ever experiencing exercise. However, foresight about which stocks will achieve such consistent price support is difficult. It takes only a single, temporary dip in price to be exposed to exercise, a risk that cannot be overlooked. Exercise is not necessarily a drastic outcome, but it does tie up your capital because it requires that you buy stock above current market value. While you wait for the stock's price to rebound, you will miss other market opportunities.

Remember the basic guideline for selling puts: You need to be willing to buy 100 shares of the underlying stock at the striking price, which you consider a fair price for that stock. If current market value is lower than striking price, you should believe that the price is going to rebound, justifying the purchase you will be required to make upon exercise. In other words, work with stocks you consider worthwhile long-term investments.

This does not mean you would necessarily welcome exercise. It only means that you would not mind buying those shares at the striking price. You might still want to avoid exercise whenever possible by rolling positions, remembering that exercise of many puts means you may end up with a portfolio of overpriced stocks.

Example

Poor Programming: You sold several puts in the past few months. This month the entire market fell several hundred points. Five of your puts were exercised at the same time, requiring you to purchase 500 shares of stock. All your available capital now is tied up in these shares. Consequently, your portfolio's basis is higher than current market value for all the shares you own. The market is recovering, but very slowly. Even considering your premium income, you are in a large paper loss position. You have no choice but to sit out the market and hope for a rebound in the future.

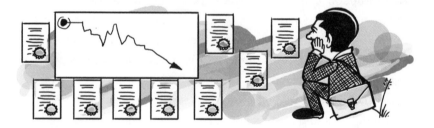

The net cost level for stock acquired through exercise of puts is the striking price, minus premiums you received when you sold the puts. Allowing for transaction fees paid (both when you sold the put and when you bought the shares), your basis will be higher still. You should not overlook the potential paper loss position you could experience in the event of a broad down-trending market. You may recover this paper loss position by selling calls on the stock you have acquired, but you also have to be careful with that strategy. Be sure that if the calls are exercised, you will not go out of the long position with a net loss. Chances are that in the event of a large market decline, you will need to wait out a recovery before making any further decisions.

Strategy 2: Using Idle Cash

When you sell options, your broker requires deposits of cash or securities. With puts, the maximum risk is identified easily. It is equal to the striking price of the put. If the short put is exercised and you are required to buy 100 shares, the firm needs to ensure that you have cash or securities available to honor the purchase.

You may hold your capital on the sidelines, believing that stocks you want to buy are overpriced and will be more attractively priced in the future. The dilemma is that the longer cash is held in reserve, the more you miss opportunities to put that money to work. Idle cash does not earn money, and there is no way to know how long it will take for conditions to present themselves, making the desired move practical.

One way to deal with this problem is by selling puts on the targeted stock. In this way, capital is still kept in reserve, yet you earn money from put premiums *and* you discount the basis in the stock in the event of exercise. You will profit from selling the put if the stock's price rises; and you will end up buying shares at the striking price (less premium discount) if the stock's market value falls. In either event, the premium you receive will be yours to keep.

When you sell options, your broker requires deposits of cash or securities. With puts, the maximum risk is identified easily. It is equal to the striking price of the put. If the short put is exercised and you are required to buy 100 shares, the firm needs to ensure that you have cash or securities available to honor the purchase.

You may hold your capital on the sidelines, believing that stocks you want to buy are overpriced and will be more attractively priced in the future. The dilemma is that the longer cash is held in reserve, the more you miss opportunities to put that money to work. Idle cash does not earn money, and there is no way to know how long it will take for conditions to present themselves, making the desired move practical.

One way to deal with this problem is by selling puts on the targeted stock. In this way, capital is still kept in reserve, yet you earn money from put premiums *and* you discount the basis in the stock in the event of exercise. You will profit from selling the put if the stock's price rises; and you will end up buying shares at the striking price (less premium discount) if the stock's market value falls. In either event, the premium you receive will be yours to keep.

Example

Planning for a Correction: You are interested in buying stock as a long-term investment. However, you believe that the current market price is too high, and that a correction is likely to occur in the near future. One possible solution: Sell one put for every 100 shares you want to buy, instead of buying the stock. Place your capital on deposit with the brokerage firm as security against your short position in the puts. If the current market value of the stock rises, your short puts will fall in value and can be closed at a profit or allowed to expire worthless. In this way, you benefit from rising market value without placing all your capital at risk.

If market value of the stock declines, you will purchase the shares at the striking price. Your basis will be discounted by the amount of premium you received for selling the puts. As a long-term investor, you will be confident that the share price will grow over time, and the current paper loss will be partially offset by the premium.

One aspect of this approach that is troubling is the possibility of lost opportunity. If you are wrong in your belief about a stock and its market value continues to rise, selling puts brings some income, but you pass up the chance to buy stock. So when you sell puts as an alternative to buying shares outright, you also need to accept this risk, or to mitigate the risk in other ways. For example, many combination strategies provide the chance to reduce lost opportunity risk while continuing to sell short options.

Strategy 3: Buying Stock

The third reason for selling puts is to intentionally seek exercise. Selling a put discounts the basis in stock in the event of exercise, and when seeking exercise, you will not be concerned with price drops in the stock.

Example

Putting It Another Way: You have been tracking a stock for several months, and you have decided that you are willing to buy 100 shares at or below $40 per share. The current price is $45. You could wait for the stock to drop to your level, which might or might not happen. However, an alternative is to sell a November 45 put, which has a current premium value of 6. This is all time value. If the market value of stock rises, the put will become worthless and the $600 you received is yours to keep. You could then repeat the transaction on the same argument as before, at a higher price increment. If the stock's market value falls below striking price, the put will be exercised. Your basis would be $39—striking price of 45 minus 6 points received in put premium—or $1 per share below your target purchase price.

SELLING PUT

In this example, the put was sold at the money and the premium—all time value—was high enough to create a net basis below your target price. Even if the stock's market value were to fall below $40 per share, your long-term plans would not be affected. You considered $40 per share a reasonable purchase level for the shares. As a long-term investor, you are not concerned with short-term price changes. Simply waiting for the right price to come along means you expose yourself to the risk of losing the opportunity to get the stock at your price. Selling puts discounts current market value and makes it worthwhile to wait for exercise, especially if you believe the current market price is inflated. For example, if a broad-based market rise has resulted in the stock's price rising quickly, the timing for the option position could be good. If time value is high in the put you're thinking of selling, it is a better alternative than buying shares of stock.

Example

Reduced Basis, Nicely Put: You are interested in buying stock at $40 per share. Current market value is $45. You sell a put with a striking price of 45 and receive 6. Willing to take exercise, you reduce your potential basis to $39 per share by selling the put. However, instead of falling, the stock's market value rose 14 points.

In this scenario, the put will expire worthless and you keep the $600 as profit. But if you had bought shares instead of selling the put, you would have earned $1,400 in profit. However, once your put expires, you are free to sell another one, offsetting the lost opportunity and perhaps exceeding that potential profit over time. The lost $1,400 is easy to recognize after the fact; however, at the time of making the decision to sell a put, you have no way of knowing whether the price will rise or fall. If share price were too high, you could risk *losing* $1,400 just as easily as you miss the opportunity for profiting by the same degree. This is why selling puts sometimes presents an attractive alternative to buying shares outright.

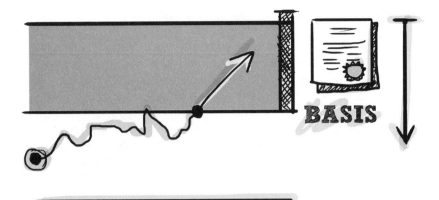

You risk losing future profits in two ways as a put seller, so you need to be willing to assume these risks in exchange for the premium income:

1. If the price of the underlying stock rises beyond the point value you received in premium, you lose the opportunity to realize profits by owning the stock. You settle for premium income only. However, when this occurs, your put expires worthless and you are free to sell another and receive additional premium.

2. If the price of the underlying stock falls significantly, you are required to buy 100 shares at the striking price, which will be above current market value. It might take considerable time for the stock's market value to rebound to the striking price level. Meanwhile, your capital is tied up in stock you bought above current market value.

Selling puts as a means for buying stock (or exposing yourself to the possibility of buying) makes sense as long as you believe the striking price is a reasonable price for that stock. If the put expires or falls in value, you profit from the short put. If it is exercised, you purchase stock at a price higher than current market value. This *contingent purchase* strategy makes sense because you can also recover the difference between striking price and market value by selling covered calls.

contingent purchase

A strategy involving the sale of a put and willingness to accept exercise, which will result in purchasing 100 shares of stock. The strategy makes sense when the individual believes the striking price is a reasonable price for the stock.

Example

From Put to Call: You sold a put on a stock that you would purchase at the striking price, based on today's values. That strike price was 30 and you received 2 ($200) for selling the put. However, after you sold the put, the stock's value fell to $26 per share and the put was exercised. You purchased 100 shares at $30 per share. Your net basis is $28 per share ($30 minus $2 you received for selling the put). You check options listings and discover that you can sell a covered call expiring in eight months for 3 ($300) and with a striking price of 27.50. If exercised, your overall profit will be $750 before calculating trading costs. The $300 received for selling the call reduces your basis to $25 per share. If the call is exercised at $27.50, you lose 2.5 points ($250), but you also gain $500 received for selling a put ($200) and a call ($300):

Purchase price of stock upon exercise of short put	$3,000
Sale price of stock upon exercise of covered call	−2,750
Net loss on stock	−250
Premium from sale of put	200
Premium from sale of call	300
Net profit	$250

While the risks of put selling are far more limited than those associated with uncovered call selling, you can also miss opportunities for profits in the event of stock price movement in either direction.

Strategy 4: Writing a Covered Put on Short Stock

While covered puts are not the same as covered calls, there is a corresponding position. If you are short 100 shares of stock, you cover that position by selling one put. (Your put is also defined as covered as long as you have cash in your brokerage account adequate to purchase shares at the striking price).

In the case of a short put accompanied by a short position in stock, profit is limited to the net difference between striking price of the put and the original price per share in the short position. However, the potential loss is a far more serious problem. If the price of stock were to increase substantially, profits in the put would not be enough to match the resulting loss in the stock. Thus, the covered put does not provide the same definition of "cover" as does the covered call.

Alternative option strategies—such as buying calls—provide better protection for those with short stock positions. In the event the stock rises in value, in-the-money calls will match the loss with dollar-for-dollar profits. In comparison, the covered put is too limited to offer any true protection against the worst-case outcome.

Strategy 5: Creating a Tax Put

A fifth reason to sell puts is to create an advantage for tax purposes, which is known as a *tax put*. However, before employing this strategy, you should consult with your tax adviser to determine that you time the transaction properly and legally, and to ensure that the tax rules have not changed. You also need to be able to identify the risks and potential liabilities involved with the tax put.

An investor who has a paper loss position on stock has the right to sell and create a capital loss at any time, even if the timing is intended to reduce income tax liability. Such losses are limited to annual maximums.

Valuable Resource
Valuable Resource: To learn more about tax puts and other rules for taxation of options, download the free book, "Taxes and Investing: A Guide for the Individual Investor," from the CBOE, at **www.cboe.com/LearnCenter/pdf/TaxesandInvesting.pdf.**

You can deduct capital losses only up to those maximums; the excess is carried over to future years. By selling puts at the same time that you take a tax loss, you offset part of that loss. The tax put is maximized when the put expiration occurs in the following tax year. (For example, expiration will occur in January or later, but you sell the put in December or earlier.) If your net stock loss is greater than the maximum allowed, the profit on

the put is absorbed by that over-the-limit loss. By selling a put when you also sell stock at a loss, one of three possible outcomes will occur:

1. The stock's market value rises and the option expires worthless. The stock loss is deducted in the year stock is sold, but profit on the short put is taxed in the following year, when it expires. This has the effect of enabling you to take stock losses in the current year but defer put premium gains until the following year.

2. The stock's market value rises and you close the position in the put, profiting by the premium difference. This creates a short-term capital gain in the year the position is closed.

3. The stock's market value falls below the striking price, and you are assigned the stock. In this case, your basis in the stock is discounted by the amount received for selling the put.

A potential problem arises in the event that the put is exercised within 30 days from the date you sold the shares of stock. Under the *wash sale rule*, you cannot claim a loss in stock if you repurchase the same stock within 30 days.

The tax put provides you with a twofold advantage. First, you take a current-year loss on stock, reducing your overall tax liability, while deferring tax on the put sale until the following tax year. Second, you profit from selling the put, as shown in Figure 6.2, in the following two ways:

1. The premium income offsets the loss in stock.

2. In the event of exercise, your basis in the stock is discounted by the put premium.

Date	Action	Received	Paid
August 15	Buy 100 shares at $50		$5,000
December 15	Sell 100 shares at $477	$4,700	
December 15	Sell 1 Feb 50 put at 6	$ 600	
	Total	$5,300	$5,000
	Net Cash	$ 300	

Price Movement	Result
Stock rises above striking price.	$300 profit.
	Put is bought at a profit.
Stock falls below striking price.	Put is exercised at $50, net cost $47 (with $300 profit from tax put).

Figure 6.2 Example of Tax Put

Put sellers enjoy an important advantage over call sellers: Put risk is not unlimited because the stock's market value can only fall so far. An example of a put write is described next and illustrated with profit and loss zones in Figure 6.3.

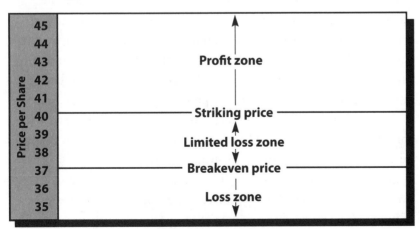

Figure 6.3 Example of Put Write with Profit and Loss Zones

Example

A Strategy with Several Aspects: You bought stock at $38 per share, and it is currently valued at $34. You sell shares in December and take a $400 loss. At the same time, you sell a March 35 put at 6. The $400 loss in stock is offset by a $600 premium from selling the put. If exercised, adjusted basis in the stock is discounted by the put premium. The put is not taxed until exercised, closed, or expired, so this also creates a tax deferral on the option side and a current write-off for loss on the stock side. (If the buyer were to exercise the put within 30 days from the date you sold stock, you would not be able to claim the loss on stock, under the wash sale rule.)

While the premium you receive for the put is yours to keep, you acquire stock above market value and you can then wait until the price rebounds. You could also absorb the paper loss on acquired stock by selling covered calls against it, further discounting your basis in the stock.

The most undesirable outcome you face as a put seller is that stock may become worthless. This is a remote possibility, but it remains within the realm of possible outcomes. You mitigate the risk by selecting stocks critically and applying fundamental tests aimed at identifying tangible value, rather than depending on popularity measures and technical indicators. The possibility only emphasizes the importance of selecting stock carefully before writing puts. In the event a stock became worthless, your put would be exercised and you would buy 100 shares at the striking price. Current market value would be zero. The more likely risk level is book value. It is always possible for a stock's market value to fall below book value. The fundamental value of a company's equity has little to do with market pricing, especially in the short term. Additionally, it is possible that reported book value has been inflated by reporting of exaggerated earnings, improper capitalizing of expenses, or underreporting of liabilities. All these potential causes for loss have to be considered as possible risks when selling puts, not to mention as risks of purchasing stock even without involving options.

Tangible net worth—assuming it is an accurate value—often is overlooked in the more important factor affecting value. The *perception* of future investment value, which might be positive or negative, directly and immediately affects current share price. Even when the fundamental strength of a company has been established, the market might discount that value to some degree. Market pricing is far from rational, and you need to keep that reality in mind. Having this knowledge gives you an advantage, because you can judge a stock's value before deciding how or whether you employ calls or puts.

You need to be willing, as a put seller, to buy 100 shares at the short put's striking price, recognizing that exercise is possible when the put is in the money. In the event of exercise, the exercise price will always be above current market value. As long as you believe that striking price is reasonable, exercise is acceptable, because short-term price movement does not affect the stock's long-term growth potential. If you believe in the company's prospects as a long-term investment, selling puts can be a smart way to increase current income while discounting your basis in the stock.

The range of choices available in buying or selling options is vast, and anyone with a stock portfolio can employ options in numerous ways. However, it remains important to pick stocks based on smart analysis, and not on rumor or name recognition. One of the big pitfalls in trading options is to pick stocks based on option premium value, while overlooking the important fundamental and technical tests.

197

CLOSING POSITIONS: COVER, CLOSE, EXERCISE, OR ROLL

7

Don't wait for the Last Judgment. It takes place every day.
—Albert Camus, *The Fall*, 1956

Every option will be canceled by an offsetting closing transaction, by exercise, or by expiration. The results of each affect buyers and sellers in different ways.

DEFINING POSSIBLE OUTCOMES OF CLOSING OPTIONS

The range of possible outcomes relies on whether you are the buyer or the seller. In many cases, an advantage to one side is going to act as a disadvantage for the other. This occurs because time value works against buyers, but in favor of sellers.

Results for the Buyer

- If you cancel your open long position with a closing sale transaction, you will receive payment. If the closing price is higher than the original purchase amount, you realize a profit; if lower, you suffer a loss.

- If you exercise the option, you will receive 100 shares (if a call) or sell 100 shares (if a put) at the striking price. You will exercise only when that action is advantageous based on current market value of the underlying stock. To justify exercise, market value has to be higher than the striking price (of a call) or lower than the striking price (of a put). At that time, you will be required to pay the striking price plus trading fees, acquiring stock below current market value.
- If you allow the option to expire, you will lose the entire amount of premium paid at the time of purchase. It will be a complete loss.

Results for the Seller

- If you cancel your open position with a closing purchase transaction, you pay the premium. If the price you pay to close is lower than the amount you received when you opened the position, you realize a profit; if it is higher, you suffer a loss.
- If your option is exercised by the buyer, you are required to deliver 100 shares of the underlying stock at the specified striking price (of a call) or to purchase 100 shares of stock at the specified striking price (of a put). As a call seller, exercise results in shares being called away. As a put seller, exercise results in shares being put to you. In either case, upon exercise, the premium you originally received for going short is yours to keep, and that adjusts your net cost.
- If the option expires worthless, you earn a profit. Your open position is canceled by expiration, and the premium you received at the time that you sold the option is yours to keep.

These outcomes are summarized in Figure 7.1. Notice that buyers and sellers have opposite results for each outcome upon close. The investor who opened the position through buying receives payment upon sale; and the investor who opened the position through selling makes payment upon a later purchase. The buyer elects to exercise, whereas the seller has no choice as to the decision, nor over the timing of exercise. If the option expires worthless, the buyer suffers a total loss, and the seller realizes a total profit.

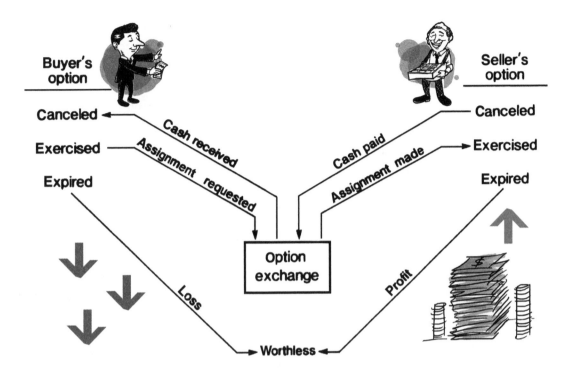

Figure 7.1 Outcomes of Closing the Position

Key Point

Analysis of the possible outcomes is the key to identifying opportunities in the options market. Risk and opportunity evaluation is imperative. Successful options traders need to be shrewd analysts.

EXERCISING THE OPTION

Option transactions occur through the exchange on which an option has been listed. While several different exchanges handle options trading, and automated trading has become widespread on the Internet (especially in options), there is but one registered clearing agency for all listed option trades in the United States. The Options Clearing Corporation (OCC) has the broad responsibility for *orderly settlement* of all option contracts, which takes place through contact between brokerage houses and customers working with the exchange. Orderly settlement means, generally, that buyer and seller both trade in confidence, knowing that they will be able to execute their orders when they want, and finding a ready market. It also means that all terms of the contract are ironclad; exercise price, expiration date, and availability of shares upon exercise are all a part of the orderly settlement. To ensure orderly settlement and in recognition of the probability that option buying and selling does not always match up, the OCC acts in the capacity of buyer to every seller, and as seller to every buyer.

Key Point

Orderly settlement is ensured even when the volume of calls and puts is out of balance; the OCC facilitates the opposite side of every option transaction.

When a customer notifies a broker and places an order for execution of an option trade, the OCC ensures that the terms of the contract will be honored. Under this system, buyer and seller do not need to depend upon the goodwill of one another; the transaction goes through the OCC, which depends upon member brokerage firms to enforce *assignment*. Remember that buyers and sellers are not matched together one-on-one. A disparate number of open buy and sell options are likely to exist at any given time, so that exercise will be meted out at random to options in the money—thus the term *assignment*. Since buyers and sellers are not matched to one another as in other types of transactions, how does a seller know whether a specific option will be exercised? There is no way to know. If your short option is in the money, exercise could occur at any time. It might not happen at all, or it might take place on the last trading day.

Valuable Resource

You will find a wealth of information about the role of OCC in options transactions, plus news, market statistics, and risk management, at the OCC website: **www.optionsclearing.com.**

When exercise occurs long before expiration date, that exercise is assigned to any of the sellers with open positions in that option. This takes place either on a random basis or on the basis of first-in, first-out (the earliest sellers are the first ones exercised). Upon exercise, 100 shares *must* be delivered. The concept of *delivery* is in relation to the movement of 100 shares of stock from the seller of the option to the exercising buyer. The buyer makes payment and receives registration of the shares, and the seller receives payment and relinquishes ownership of the shares.

OCC   **SELLER**

What happens if the seller does not deliver shares as demanded by the terms of the option contract? The OCC facilitates the market and enforces assignment. The buyer is given timely possession of 100 shares of stock, even when the seller is unwilling or unable to comply. The broker will deal with the seller by attaching other assets as necessary, or taking legal action, as well as suspending the seller's trading privileges. The buyer would have no awareness of these events if they occur, because the problem is between the violating seller and the system of broker, exchange, and the OCC. So orderly settlement ensures that everyone trading in options in good faith experiences a smooth, dependable system in which terms of the option contract are honored automatically and without fail.

When a buyer decides to exercise, 100 shares are either purchased from ("called from") or sold to ("put to") the option seller. When you have sold a call, exercise means your 100 shares could be called away and transferred to the buyer; and when you sell a put, exercise means that 100 shares of stock can be "put to" you upon exercise, meaning you are required to buy. The entire process of calling and putting shares of stock upon exercise is broadly referred to as *conversion*. Stock is assigned at the time of exercise, a necessity because the number of buyers and sellers in a particular option will rarely, if ever, match. The assignment of an option's exercise, by definition, means that 100 shares of stock are *called away*.

Is exercise always seen as a negative to the seller? At first glance, it would appear that being exercised is undesirable, and it often is seen that way; many sellers take steps to minimize the risk of exercise or to avoid it altogether. However, the question really depends upon the seller's intentions at the time he or she entered the short position. For example, a seller might recognize that being exercised at a specific price is desirable, and will be willing to take exercise with the benefit of also keeping the premium as a profit.

Key Point

Some sellers enter into a short position in the hopes that exercise will occur, recognizing that the combination of capital gain on the stock and option premium represents a worthwhile profit.

early exercise

The act of exercising an option prior to expiration date.

It is logical that most sellers will close out their short positions or pick options the least likely to be exercised. Sellers have to be aware that exercise is one possible outcome and that it can occur at any time that the option is in the money. The majority of exercise actions are most likely to occur at or near expiration, so the risk of *early exercise* is minimal, although it can and does occur.

Exercise is not always generated by a buyer's action, either. The Options Clearing Corporation can execute an *automatic exercise* on options in the money on expiration date. The OCC, acting in the role of buyer on the other side of the short position, would benefit from exercise of in-the-money short options. Automatic exercise occurs because in-the-money short positions are not necessarily exercised by buyers; it is more likely that positions will be closed and profits taken. So outstanding in-the-money short positions are automatically exercised by the OCC to absorb the disparity between the two sides.

Example

The Early Worm: You sold a call with more than six months until expiration. Confident that exercise would not occur until close to expiration, you were not concerned about the possibility. But in the last few days, the stock's market value rose dramatically. You were taken by surprise when you received notice that your call had been exercised early. The lesson to remember from this applies to all option sellers: exercise can occur any time the option is in the money.

The decision to avoid exercise is made based on current market value as well as the time remaining until expiration. Many option sellers spend a great deal of time and effort avoiding exercise and trying to also avoid taking losses in open option positions. A skilled options trader can achieve this by exchanging one option for another, and by timing actions to maximize deteriorating time value while still avoiding exercise. As long as options remain out of the money, there is no practical risk of exercise. But once that option goes in the money, sellers have to decide whether to risk exercise or cancel the position with an offsetting transaction.

Example

Reasonable Assumptions: You bought 100 shares of stock several months ago for $57 per share. You invested $5,700 plus transaction fees. Last month, the stock's market value was $62 per share. At that time, you sold a call with a striking price of 60 ($60 per share). You were paid a premium of 7 ($700). You were willing to assume this short position. Your reasoning: If the call were exercised, your profit would be $1,000 before transaction fees. That would consist of 3 points per share of profit in the stock plus the $700 you were paid for selling the option.

Striking price	$60
Less your cost per share	−57
Stock profit	$3
Option premium	+7
Total profit per share	$10

Valuable Resource

Entering positions specifically to create exercise is a valid strategy in some circumstances. But be aware of how the tax rules can affect capital gains treatment of stock when you write deep in-the-money calls. Check the Options Clearing Corporation (OCC) and download their guide to taxes and options: **www.theocc.com/components/docs/about/ publications/taxes_and_investing.pdf**.

The Reasonable Assumptions example shows that it is possible for an investor to sell an in-the-money call, hoping for exercise. The key is in the profit made combining high option premium with a profit on the stock. The premium on the option effectively discounts your basis in the stock, so that exercise creates a nice profit. If the stock's market value falls below striking price and remains there until, exercise the profit in the example is still $700 from option premium; and you would be free to wait out price movement and repeat the process again.

Example

Repetitive Strategies: You bought 100 shares of stock several months ago for $57 per share. You invested $5,700 plus transaction fees. Last month, the stock's market value was $62 per share. At that time, you sold a call with a striking price of 60, and you were paid a premium of 7 ($700). By expiration, the stock had fallen to $58 per share, and the call expired worthless. At this point, your adjusted basis in the stock is $50 per share ($57 per share paid at purchase less your profit from selling a call and receiving a premium of $700). After the call expires, you sell another call with a striking price of 55 and receive 6. If this option were to be exercised, you would realize an adjusted profit of $1,100 ($500 profit on stock plus $600 profit from selling the call). If the option's time value declines, you can sell the option and realize the difference as profit. If the option expires worthless, you can repeat the process a *third* time, realizing yet more profit, and continue that pattern indefinitely.

A word of caution: Selling in-the-money calls can affect how profits are taxed. If you have owned shares of stock long enough that a sale would be taxed at favorable long-term capital gain rates, selling an in-the-money call might reset the calculation period to zero.

The decision to act or to wait depends on the time value involved, and on the proximity of the striking price to the market value of the stock. As a general rule, the greater the time until expiration, the higher the time value will be; and the closer the striking price is to market value of the stock, the more important the time value becomes, both to buyer and to seller. For the buyer, time value is a negative, so the higher the time value, the greater the risk. For the seller, the opposite is true. Buyers pay the time value (the amount above intrinsic value) as the difference between the stock's *current market value* and the option's striking price, knowing that this time value will disappear by expiration. The seller picks options to sell with the same thing in mind, but recognizing that more time value means more potential profit.

Example

Quick Changes Artist: You have decided to buy a call with a striking price of 30. The underlying stock's current market value is $32 per share and the option premium is 5 ($500). Your premium includes 2 points of intrinsic value and 3 points of time value. If the stock's market value does not increase enough by expiration to offset your cost, then you will not be able to earn a profit. One of two things needs to happen in this situation. Either the stock's current market value needs to rise quickly so that your call premium will be greater than the 5 you paid, or the stock's market value has to rise enough points by expiration to offset time value (3 points) plus grow beyond the intrinsic value level.

TIME VALUE

SELLER   GREATER TIME OF EXPIRY   BUYER

This shows how option buyers need to evaluate risk. In the example, time value represents three-fifths of the total premium. If expiration comes up quickly, the stock will need to increase significantly in a short period of time to produce a profit. In thinking about whether it makes sense to buy such a call, consider these alternatives, especially if you believe that the stock will rise in value:

- Buy 100 shares of the stock. If you believe it has potential to increase in value, owning the shares without the built-in deadline of expiration makes ownership more desirable. The added problem of time value could translate to making outright stock purchase not only safer, but more profitable as well.

- Sell a put instead of buying a call. Put sellers have limited exposure compared to call sellers; and if the stock's market price rises, the entire premium will represent profit. Compared to buying a call, the selling of a put often is an overlooked strategy that could make a lot of sense. If you decide to sell a put, your brokerage firm will require you to deposit cash as a reserve in case of exercise, to ensure the money is available to pay for the stock. Going short is a higher-level strategy, too, so your brokerage firm may take a harder look at you and your qualifications to engage in short option strategies.
- Buy calls with more point distance between striking price and current market value. This enables you to pay less for the call, but also makes the odds of profit more difficult.
- Buy calls with longer time until expiration. While this costs more, it leaves the exposure period longer as well, so that your chances of the call's becoming profitable will be greater.

A third opportunity could present itself in taking the opposite approach to buying. Given the previous example, in which significant increase in value would be required to make a profit, it might be viewed as an opportunity to sell a call instead of buying one—as long as you remember the higher risks that are involved. Selling uncovered calls is one of the highest-risk strategies you can use; risk is unlimited, at least in theory. So if you take this route, you will be assuming a much greater risk profile. Call sellers benefit from decline in time value; but uncovered short sales are the highest-risk strategies so, even with attractive profit possibilities, the risks cannot be ignored.

Example

Turning the Tables: Given the same circumstances as those in the previous example, you decide to sell a call instead of buying one. Instead of paying the $500 premium, you receive $500 as a seller. Of this, $300 represents time value, which now is an advantage rather than a problem. The possibility of expiration is an advantage as well. The pending expiration places pressure for time value to evaporate, meaning greater profits for you as a seller. As long as the stock's current market value does not increase more than 3 points between now and expiration, the transaction will be profitable. However, because the call is in the money, you also face the possibility of exercise. The 2 points of intrinsic value have to be weighed against the 5 points you receive for the call to make a value judgment about this strategy; in addition, your trading costs have to be factored into the calculation.

By the time of expiration, all of the time value will have disappeared from the premium, and all remaining premium will represent intrinsic value only. To avoid exercise, you would want to buy to close the call and take the $300 profit; however, exercise can occur at any time, so in this position you remain exposed to that possibility. When no time value remains at expiration, the condition is known as *parity*.

TIMING THE DECISION

Exercise can occur at any time that your call is in the money. It is more likely to occur close to expiration date, but you need to be prepared to give up 100 shares of stock at any time the short option remains open. This is the contractual agreement you enter when you sell the call.

Key Point

Whenever you sell a covered call, be prepared for exercise at any time when the call is in the money. The covered call strategy makes sense only if you are willing to have your 100 shares called away.

As shown in Figure 7.2, during the life of a call, the underlying stock might swing several points above or below striking price. If you own 100 shares and are thinking of selling a covered call, keep these points in mind:

- When the striking price of the call is higher than the original price you paid for the stock, exercise is not a negative; it automatically triggers a triple profit—from appreciation of the stock, call premium, and dividend income.
- If you sell a call for a striking price below your original cost of stock, be sure the premium you receive is greater than the loss you will experience in the stock in the event of exercise.
- In calculating potential yields, be sure to allow for trading costs on both stock and option, and for both entering and leaving the positions.
- For the benefit of producing a consistent profit from writing calls, remember that you give up the potential for greater gains if and when the stock's current market value rises.
- The tax consequences of covered call writing have to be included in your calculation, especially if you have a substantial paper gain in the stock and have owned that stock long enough

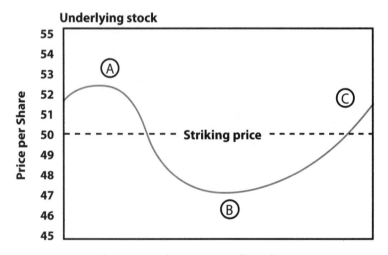

A. In the money—best time to sell a call.
B. Out of the money—best time to buy a call.
C. In the money at expiration—calls will be exercised.

Figure 7.2 Timing of Call Transactions Relative to Price Movement of Underlying Stock

that gains would be long term. In instances when you write in-the-money calls against stock, you could lose the long-term status of stock, so tax planning has to be a part of your strategy unless you restrict your short positions to out-of-the-money contracts.

In this example, the premium contains only 3 points of intrinsic value. The 4 points of time value indicates the probability of a long time to go to expiration. Selling a call in this case provides several advantages to you:

- If the stock's current market value falls below your purchase price, you can buy the option and close the position at a profit, or wait for it to expire worthless.
- By selling the call, you discount your basis in the stock from $51 to $44 per share, providing yourself with 7 points of downside protection. In the event of a price decline in the stock's market value, this is a substantial degree of protection.
- You continue to receive dividends as long as the option is not exercised.

You can also choose to sell a covered call that is deep in the money, as long as you are aware of the tax consequences of that decision.

Example

Alternative to Selling: You buy 100 shares of stock at $51 per share, and it rises to $53. Rather than sell the stock, you choose to sell a call with a striking price of 50, and you are paid a premium of 7.

Example

Going Deep: You bought stock at $51 per share and it is now worth $53. You will receive a premium of at least 8 if you sell a call with a striking price of 45 (because there would be 8 points of intrinsic value). That also increases the chances of exercise substantially. For the 8 points in intrinsic premium, you would lose 6 points in the stock upon exercise (your original basis of $51 less exercise price of $45). These outcomes would change if time value were also available. For example, a 45 call might have current premium of 11, with the additional 3 points representing time value. Upon exercise, the additional 3 points would represent additional profit: $1,100 for selling the call, minus a loss of $600 on the stock, for a net profit of $500 upon exercise. The tax consequences have to be calculated as well. A long-term gain could be subject to short-term treatment for writing deep-in-the-money calls.

Key Point

Selling deep-in-the-money calls can produce high profits for call sellers, especially if they want to sell their stock anyway.

This is not an unreasonable method for producing profits. The outcome occurs only if the call is exercised; in the event the stock's market value falls, the call premium falls one dollar for each dollar lost in the stock's market value. You can buy the call to close the position, with the profit discounting your basis in the stock. Once the position has been closed at a profit, you can repeat the strategy, further reducing your basis in the stock. There is no limit as to how many times you can sell covered calls after a closing purchase, or after expiration.

Example

Exercise of Fast Profits: You bought shares of stock at $51 per share, and it is worth $53 at the time that you sell a 45 call. You receive a premium of 11. The market value of the stock later falls 3 points, to $50 per share. The call is worth 7, representing a drop of 3 points of intrinsic value and 1 point of time value. You can close the position and buy the call for 7, realizing a $400 profit. You still own the stock and are free to sell covered calls again.

Always select options and time covered call sales with these considerations in mind:

- The original price per share of the stock.
- The premium you will be paid for selling the call.
- The mix between intrinsic value and time value.
- The gap between current market value of the stock and striking price of the call.
- The time until expiration.
- Total return if the call is exercised, compared to total return if the option expires worthless.
- Your objective in owning the stock (long-term growth, for example), compared to your objective in selling the call (immediate income and downside protection, for example).

Key Point

Be aware of ex-dividend date as a likely time for early exercise of calls. If the call is in the money, exercise might occur so that the buyer can earn the dividend.

AVOIDING EXERCISE

If you sell a call on stock originally purchased as a long-term investment, you might want to take steps to avoid exercise. This is not contradictory; as a specific strategy, you can write covered calls with the willingness to accept exercise, but with a preference to avoid it. If your primary purpose is to hold stock as a long-term investment, covered call selling enhances current income without necessarily requiring that you give up stock. The overall guideline remains the same: Never sell a covered call unless you are willing to go through exercise and give up 100 shares of stock at the striking price. The strategy is twofold: If you would prefer to keep the stock for long-term investment growth, you need to view calls as current income generators, while also accepting the possibility that the calls might be exercised.

Call sellers—even after picking strategies well—may experience a rise in the stock and later wish to avoid exercise, in order to (a) achieve higher potential capital gains, (b) augment call premium income, and (c) put off selling a stock that is increasing in value.

You avoid exercise in two primary ways: by canceling the option or by rolling out of one option and replacing it with another. The following examples are all based on a situation in which unexpected upward price movement occurs in the underlying stock, placing you in the position where exercise is likely.

Example

Paper Profit Problems: You sold a May 35 call on stock when the stock's market value was $34 per share. The stock's current market value is $41, and you would like to avoid exercise to take advantage of the higher market value of the stock.

Method 1: Cancel the option. You can cancel the option by purchasing it. Although this creates a loss in the option, it is offset by a corresponding increase in the value of the stock. If time value has declined, this strategy makes sense—especially if the increased value of stock exceeds the loss in the option.

Example

Short-Term Loss, Long-Term Gain: You bought 100 shares of stock at $21 per share and later sold a June 25 call for 4. The stock's current market value is $30 per share and the call's premium is at 6. If you buy the call, you will lose $200; however, by getting around exercise, you avoid having to sell the $30 stock at $25 per share. You now own 100 shares at $30, and are free to sell an option with a higher striking price, if you want.

In this example, the outcome can be summarized in two ways. First, remember that by closing the call position at a loss, you still own the 100 shares of stock. That frees you to sell another call with a striking price of 30 or higher, which would create more option premium. (If you could sell a new option for 2 or more, it offsets your loss in the June 25 call.)

You can also analyze the transaction by comparing the exercise price of the option to the outcome of closing the option and selling shares at current market value. The flaw in this method is that it assumes a sale of stock, which is not necessarily going to occur; however, the comparison is valuable to determine whether avoiding exercise makes sense. A summary:

	Exercise	Sale
Basis in 100 shares of stock	−2,100	−2,100
Call premium received	400	400
Call premium paid		−600
100 shares deliver at $25	2,500	
100 shares sold at $30	2,500	3,000
Net profit	$800	$700

This comparison appears to conclude that you have a better outcome by allowing exercise of the call. That is a fair conclusion only if you would be willing to give up the 100 shares; but it excludes two very important considerations. First, upon exercise you have a capital gain on the stock and a tax consequence. Second, if you keep stock you are free to write covered calls again after expiration or close of the current positions, meaning more income in the future. Exercise ends that possibility.

Key Point

A careful comparison between choices is the only way to decide whether to accept exercise or to close out the whole position.

roll-forward

The replacement of one written call with another with the same striking price, but a later expiration date.

Method 2: Roll options to avoid exercise. A second technique to avoid exercise involves exchanging one option for another, while making a profit or avoiding a loss in the exchange. Since the premium value for a new option will be greater if more time value is involved until expiration, you can trade on that time value. Such a strategy is likely to defer exercise even when the call is in the money, when you remember that the majority of exercise decisions are made close to expiration date. This technique is called a *roll-forward*.

Example

Trading Expirations: The May 40 call you wrote against 100 shares of stock is near expiration and is in the money. To avoid or delay exercise, you close the May 40 option by buying it; and you immediately sell an August 40 call—this has the same striking price but a later expiration.

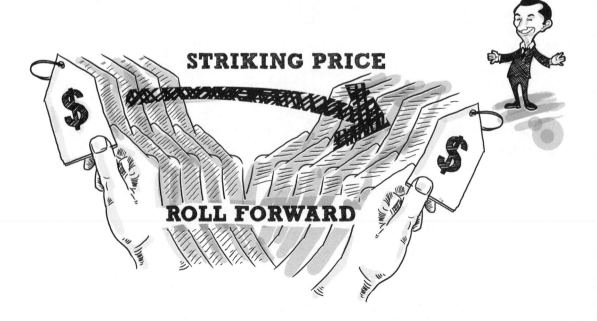

You still face the risk of exercise at any time; however, it is less likely with a call three months further out. In addition, if you believe that expiration is inevitable, this strategy provides you with additional income. Because the August 40 call has more time until expiration, it also has more time value premium. The roll-forward can be used whether you own a single call or several. The more lots of 100 shares you own of the underlying stock, the greater your flexibility in rolling forward and adding to your option premium profits. Canceling a single call and rolling forward produces a marginal gain; however, if you cancel one call and replace it with two or more later-expiring calls, your gain will be greater. For example, you own 300 shares and have previously sold one call; you can roll forward, replacing one call with either two or three which expire later. This strategy is called *incremental return*. Profits increase as you increase the number of calls sold against stock.

incremental return

A technique for avoiding exercise while increasing profits with written calls. When the value of the underlying stock rises, a single call is closed at a loss and replaced with two or more call writes with later expiration dates, producing cash and a net profit in the exchange.

Example

Avoiding Exercise with More Cash: You own 300 shares of stock that you bought for $31 per share. You sold one call with a striking price of 35, and received a premium of 4. Now the stock is worth $39 per share and you would like to avoid or delay exercise. You buy the original call and pay 8, accepting a loss of $400, and replace it by selling three 35 calls with a later expiration for 4 each, receiving a total premium of 12. The net transaction yields you an extra $400 in cash: $1,200 for the three calls, minus $800 paid to close the original position.

In this example, you trade exposure on 100 shares of stock for exposure on 300 shares, but you avoid or delay exercise as well. At the same time, you net out additional cash profits, which reduces your overall basis in the stock. This makes exercise more acceptable later on. Of course, you can continue to use rolling techniques to avoid exercise. Another important point worth evaluating is the potential tax advantage or consequence. Options are taxed in the year that positions are closed; so when you roll forward, you recognize a loss in the original call transaction, which can be deducted on your current year's federal income tax return. At the same time, by rolling forward you receive a net payment while deferring profits, perhaps to the following year. However, because the roll-forward may involve in-the-money positions, the stock profit may revert to a short-term gain instead of the more favorable long-term gain.

roll-down

The replacement of one written call with another that has a lower striking price.

The roll-forward maintains the same striking price and buys you time, which makes sense when the stock's value has gone up. However, the plan does not always suit the circumstances. Another rolling method is called the *roll-down*.

Example

Repetitive Profits: You originally bought 100 shares of stock at $31 per share, and later sold a call with a striking price of 35, for a premium of 3. The stock has fallen in value and your call now is worth 1. You cancel (buy) the call and realize a profit of $200, and immediately sell a call with a striking price of 30, receiving a premium of 4.

If the option is exercised at its striking price of 30, the net loss in the stock will be $100; but your net profit in option premium would be $600, so your overall profit would be $500:

Striking price of shares	$3,000
Less original price of shares	−3,100
Loss on stock	−100
Profit on first call sold	200
Profit on second call sold	400
Net profit	$500

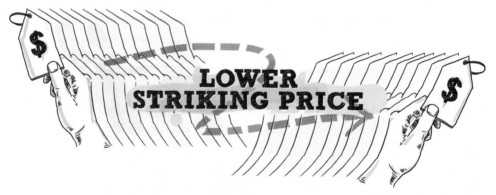

The roll-down is an effective way to offset losses in stock positions in a declining market, as long as the price decline is not severe. Profits in the call premium offset losses to a degree, reducing your basis in the stock. This works as long as the point drop in stock does not exceed the offset level in call premium. You face a different problem in a rising market, where the likelihood of exercise motivates you to take steps to move from in-the-money to out-of-the-money status, or to reduce the degree of in-the-money. In that situation, you may use the *roll-up*.

Example

Trading Losses for Profits: You originally paid $31 per share for 100 shares of stock, and later sold a call with a striking price of 35. The stock's current market value has risen to $39 per share. You cancel (buy) the call and accept a loss, offsetting that loss by selling another call with a striking price of 40 and more time to go until expiration.

roll-up

The replacement of one written call with another that has a higher striking price.

With this technique, the loss in the original call can be replaced by the premium in the new call. With more time to go until expiration, the net cash difference is in your favor. This technique depends on time value to make it profitable. In some cases, the net difference will be minimal or may even cost money. However, considering you will be picking up an extra 5 points in the striking price by avoiding exercise, you can afford a loss in the roll-up as long as it does not exceed that 5-point difference.

Key Point

Rolling techniques can help you to maximize option returns without going through exercise, most of the time. But the wise seller is always prepared to give up shares. That is the nature of selling options.

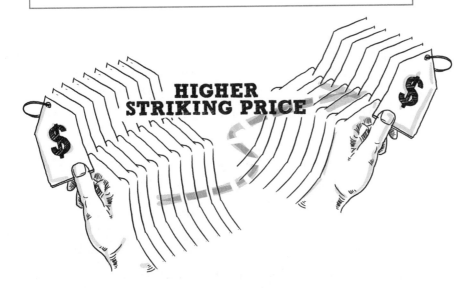

It is conceivable that the various rolling techniques can be used indefinitely to avoid exercise, while continuing to produce profits. Figure 7.3 provides one example of how this could occur.

Example

Staying Ahead of the Curve: You own 800 shares of stock that you bought at $30 per share; your basis is $24,000. You expect the value of the stock to rise, but you also want to write covered calls and increase profits while providing yourself with downside protection. So on March 15, you sell two June 30 contracts for 5 apiece, and receive payment of $1,000.

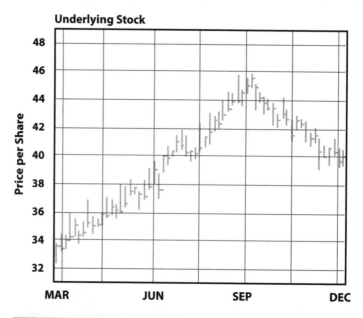

Date	Description	Received	Paid
Mar 15	Buy 100 shares at $50.	$1,000	
Jun 11	Buy 2 Jun 30 calls at 8. Sell 5 Sep 35 calls at 6.	$3,000	$1,600
Sep 8	Buy 5 Sep 35 calls at 9. Sell 8 Dec 40 calls at 6.	$4,800	$4,500
Dec 22	Dec 40 calls expire worthless.	–	
	Totals	$8,800	$6,100
	Profit	$2,700	

Figure 7.3 Using the Rolling Technique to Avoid Exercise

On June 11, the stock's market value is at $38 per share. To avoid exercise, you close the two calls by buying them, paying a premium of 8 each (total paid, $1,600). You replace these calls with five September 35 calls and receive 6 for each, getting a total of $3,000.

On September 8, the stock's market value has risen again, and now is valued at $44 per share. You want to avoid exercise again, so you cancel your open positions and pay a premium of 9 each, or $4,500 total. You sell eight December 40 calls in replacement at 6 each, and you receive a total of $4,800.

By December 22, the day of expiration, the stock has fallen to $39 per share. Your eight outstanding calls expire worthless. Your total profit on this series of transactions is $2,700 in net call premium. In addition, you still own 800 shares of stock, now worth $39 per share, which is nine points or a total of $7,200 above your original basis. If you wish, you can begin selling calls again, now that all short positions have expired.

For the volume of transactions, you might wonder if the exposure to exercise was worth the $2,700 in profit. It certainly was, considering that the strategy here was dictated by rising stock prices. While you received a profit on call options premium, you also avoided exercise as prices rose. Upon expiration of the calls, you are free to repeat the process. The incremental return combining roll-up and roll-forward demonstrates how you can avoid exercise while still generating a profit. You cannot depend on this pattern to continue or to repeat, but strategies can be devised based on the situation. It helps, too, that the example involves multiple lots of stock, providing flexibility in writing calls.

This example is based on the premise that you would have been happy to accept exercise at any point along the way. Certainly, exercise would always have been profitable, considering original cost of shares, option premium, and striking prices. If you were to sell the 800 shares at the ending market value of $39 per share, total profit would have been substantial using covered calls, with 41.25 percent profit based on original cost of the stock:

Stock	
Sell 800 shares at $39	$31,200
Less original cost	−24,000
Profit on stock	$7,200
Options	
Sell 2 June contracts	$1,000
Buy 2 June contracts	−1,600
Sell 5 September contracts	3,000
Buy 5 September contracts	−4,500
Sell 8 December contracts	4,800
Profit on options	$2,700
Total profit	$9,900
Yield	41.25%

Whenever you roll forward, higher time value is a benefit. Greater premium value is found in calls with the same striking price but more time before expiration. The longer the time involved, the higher your potential future income from selling the call. In exchange for the higher income, you agree to remain exposed to the risk of exercise for a longer period of time. You are locked into the striking price until you close the position, go through exercise, or wait out expiration.

Key Point

The key to profiting from rolling forward is in remembering that the longer the time until expiration, the more time value there will be in the call.

Example

Rolling Along: You own 200 shares of stock originally purchased at $40 per share. You are open on a short June 40 call, which you sold for 3. The stock currently is worth $45 per share, and you want to avoid being exercised at $40. Table 7.1 shows current values of calls that are available on this stock. A review of this table provides you several alternatives for using rolling techniques.

Your strategies to defer or avoid exercise combine two dissimilar goals: increasing your option income while also holding on to the stock, even when market value is above striking price. This can be achieved through profiting from higher time value, in recognition of the probability that options will not be exercised until closer to expiration date. Most exercise occurs at or near expiration.

Table 7.1 Current Call Option Values

	Expiration Month		
Striking Price	**June**	**Sept.**	**Dec.**
35	11	13	15
40	6	8	10
45	1	2	5

Strategy 1: Rolling up and forward. Sell one December 45 call at 5 while closing out the original June 40 call at 6. This produces a net cash payout of $100, but puts you at the money, removing the immediate risk of exercise. Because the striking price of the new short position is five poin higher, you will earn $500 more in profit if the new call is eventually exercised.

Strategy 2: Rolling with incremental return. Sell two September 45 cal while closing the June 40 call at 6, producing $200 cash difference. Y receive $400 for the two new short calls, versus the $600 you pay to the original call. Now you are at the money on two calls, instead of bei in the money on one.

Strategy 3: Rolling forward only. Sell one September 40 call at 8 while closing the June 40 call at 6, resulting in net cash received of $200. You're still in the money, but you increase premium income by 2 points.

Note in these strategies that we refer to the loss on the June call. Because that call currently is valued at 6, it requires a cash outlay of $600 to close the position. You received $300 when you sold, so your net loss is $300.

The loss of $300 is acceptable in all of these strategies because either the call with striking price of 40 is replaced with a call with a striking price of 45, which is 5 points higher, or additional income is produced to offset that loss by replacing the call with others that will expire later.

If the underlying stock is reasonably stable—for example, if its market value tends to stay within a 5-point range during a typical three-month period—it is possible to employ rolling techniques and avoid exercise indefinitely, as long as no early exercise occurs. As stated before, however, you have to remember that when your short positions are in the money, exercise can occur at any time. Rolling techniques are especially useful when stocks break out of their short-term trading ranges and you want to take advantage of increased market value while also profiting from selling calls—while also avoiding exercise.

To demonstrate how such a strategy can work, refer to Table 7.2. This shows a series of trades over a period of two years, and is a summary of a series of trades taken from actual confirmation receipts. The investor owned 400 shares of stock. Sale and purchase price show actual amounts of cash transacted including brokerage fees, rounded to the nearest dollar. The total net profit of $2,628 involved $722 in brokerage charges, so that profits before those charges were $3,350.

Table 7.2 Selling Calls with Rolling Techniques

| Calls | Type | Sold | | Bought | | | |
		Date	Amount	Date	Amount	Profit	Notes
Traded	Jul 35	3/20	$328	4/30	$221	$107	
1	Oct 35	6/27	235	10/8	78	157	
1	Apr 35	1/15	247	4/14	434	−187	
1	Oct 35	4/14	604	6/24	228	376	1
1	Oct 35	7/31	353	9/12	971	−618	
1	Jan 45	9/12	915	12/16	172	743	2
2	Apr 45	12/16	379	2/24	184	195	
2	Jul 40	3/9	1,357	5/26	385	972	3
4	Oct 40	6/5	1,553	7/22	1,036	517	
4	Jan 40	8/5	1,504	9/15	1,138	366	
		Totals	$7,475		$4,847	$2,628	

[1] A roll-forward: The loss on the April 35 call was acceptable to avoid exercise, since the October 35 was profitable.
[2] A combination roll-forward and roll-up: The loss on the October 35 call was acceptable to avoid exercise at a low striking price. The number of calls was incrementally increased from one to two.
[3] A roll-down combined with an incremental return: The number of calls changed from two to four, and the striking price of 45 was replaced with one for 40.

Key Point

Stocks whose options offer greater time value do so for a reason. As a general rule, those stocks are higher-risk investments.

You will be less likely to succeed if you buy overpriced stocks that later fall below your basis. No call seller wants to be exercised at a level below the basis in the stock. A comparison of risks between uncovered and covered calls is instructive. Check Figure 7.4. This shows the profit and loss zones for an uncovered call write. In this case, a single May 40 call was sold for 2. This strategy exposes the investor to unlimited risk. If the stock rises above the striking price and then exceeds the two points equal to the amount received in premium, losses rise point for point with the stock. Upon exercise, this investor will have to deliver 100 shares of stock at $40 per share, regardless of the current market value at that time.

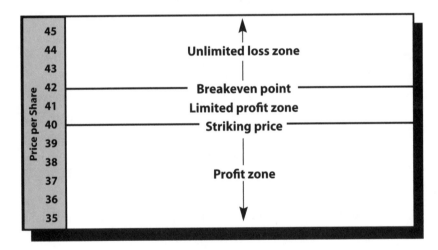

Figure 7.4 Example of Uncovered Call Write with Profit and Loss Zones

The example of a covered call write shown in Figure 7.5 demonstrates that the loss zone exists only on the downside, so the covered strategy has a much different profile than the uncovered call strategy. In this example, the investor owned 100 shares of stock that originally were purchased at $38 per share. The investor then sold a May 40 call for 2. This discounts the basis in stock by $2 per share, down to $36. As long as the stock's market value is at or below the striking price of 40, exercise will not occur. If the stock's market value rises above $40 per share, the call will be exercised and the 100 shares called away at $40 per share. In the event of exercise, profit would be $400—$200 in profit on the stock plus $200 for call premium.

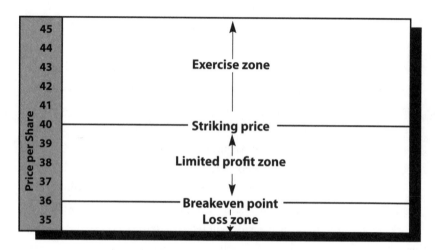

Figure 7.5 Example of Covered Call Write with Profit and Loss Zones

Rolling up, forward, or down makes sense as long as you (1) create a net credit in the exchange of cash and (2) defer or avoid exercise. Two important points to remember, however, about rolling:

1. *You can create a tax problem if you don't keep the rules in mind.* The idea of rolling forward makes sense as long as the striking price of the new option is close to the current market value of the stock. But the federal tax rules include an oddity, and rolling can create unintended consequences if you are not aware of it. Rolling involves two separate transactions, closing out a previous short option and opening up a new one. Under the federal rules, if the covered call you open today (even if it is part of a rolling strategy) is in the money by more than one increment (usually 5 points, sometimes less), you could lose the long-term capital gains treatment on your stock. So in rolling forward, make sure you don't jeopardize the status of your long-term capital gains if and when stock is called away.

2. *It sometimes makes sense to lose a little now to avoid exercise.* The concept of cutting your losses applies to covered calls as well as to any other kind of investment strategy. For example, if you sold a covered call with a striking price of 30 when the stock was at $28 per share, that was a sensible move. But if the stock has since moved up to $34 per share, your covered call

is likely to be exercised. At the time you entered the strategy, you were aware of this possibility, and you accepted the risk. But now, you would like to avoid exercise by rolling up. For example, you may be willing to close your 30 call and replace it with a 35 call expiring later. In some cases, you will not be able to achieve this exchange without spending a little more (to close the previous call) than you receive (to open the new call). So you have to make a decision. Considering that the roll-up increases potential exercise price by 5 points ($500), is it worth the loss in the two-part rolling transaction? If the net difference is only $100, it could be worth the loss to "buy" 5 points in future exercise level. This also gets you away from the in-the-money exposure, if only by a single point.

If you do decide to exchange one option for another and take a small net loss, remember to track the net difference for the net call. Its net basis will not be what you sold it for, but the net between its sale price and the loss you took on the previous call. For example, if you sold the first call and received 2 ($200) and later closed it at 3 ($300), you have a net loss on $100. But you then open a new covered call at 1.50 ($150) with a strike price five points higher and exercise three months later. Your net basis in the new covered call is 0.50 ($50). The premium you received of $150 has to be reduced by the net loss on the previous call of $100. In this situation, you have reduced the overall option premium to $50 in exchange for a 5-point increase in the strike price.

This example makes the point that timing and selection of the best striking price are crucial to the long-term success of your covered call program. If you pick stocks based on richness of time value premium, you should know ahead of time that you are exposing yourself to greater volatility; if you pick stocks with very narrow trading ranges, option premiums will be low as well. Either strategy has its good points, but it's crucial to know ahead of time what level of risk you will face. You can cover a short call and transform a high-risk strategy to a very conservative strategy. The task is not quite as easy for short put writing. The next chapter explains how this works and demonstrates how put writing can be very profitable or advantageous in a number of different ways.

229

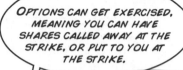

PAPER TRADING: A TEST RUN OF THE THEORY

CHAPTER 8

A verbal contract isn't worth the paper it's written on.
—Samuel Goldwyn, quoted in Laurence J. Peter, *Peter's Quotations*, 1977

Risk is present in all forms of investing. One of the troubling aspects to any new investing idea is this basic risk, and with options the lack of knowledge or experience adds to the overall risk. Anything new you try invariably will involve placing money on the line, even when you lack the experience to know for sure that the concepts will actually be profitable. So anyone new to options trading faces a dilemma: How do you gain experience without placing capital at unacceptable risks? And how do you know if a risk is acceptable until you try a trade for the first time?

This problem keeps many people away from options altogether. Few traders are willing to gain actual experience if that means losing money along the way. Few people will simply acknowledge that loss is the price they pay to gain experience; in fact, the experience you are able to gain profitably is far more satisfying. But even if you are dubious about options trading due to misunderstood or unknown risk, there is an easy solution. You can educate yourself about a variety of trading strategies, even the most exotic ones, by using a free service offered on many financial websites. This feature, called *paper trading*, lets you place trades with a fictitious starting portfolio of cash and see how it comes out.

Key Point

Paper trading works best when it simulates a real-world environment. This should include limitations on portfolio size, timing, risk, and level of transaction you are allowed to execute.

Different websites offer you a variety of features for paper trading. Selection criteria should include the following:

- *Ease of use.* The most important feature for any website is how easy it is to use. No one enjoys having to struggle with a complex or slow website. Later in this chapter, several sites are reviewed that offer a variety of easy-to-use features.
- *Realism.* Your paper trading experience should approximate the real trading environment as much as possible. Rules should apply just as they do in your trading account with a broker.
- *Trading-level distinctions.* In the real world, brokers will assign you a trading level based on your knowledge and experience and also on the cash level in your account and volume of trading activity. A paper-trading website should provide you with one of two trading capabilities. First, if you use a site that restricts your trading activity, you will learn to function within your level of experience. Second, if you are allowed to execute any risk level of trade, you will quickly learn firsthand about risk and how some options theories end up being very costly. So pick a site that provides you with the level of experience you seek—realistic based on your knowledge level, or unlimited based on your desire to try even advanced and exotic strategies.
- *Ability to trade both stocks and options.* You want a paper-trading site to provide you with a realistic trading environment, even though you will be making only mock trades. In order for paper trading to provide you with valuable experience, it should be as close as possible to the real world of stock and options trading. You should be allowed to trade both, so that you can experience the cash limitations, risk dynamics, and interaction between stocks and option values.

- *Provision of valuable support services.* A site offering paper trading is most valuable when it offers additional services. These include educational services, such as publications, articles, and useful links. Many sites have options glossaries or bookstores, links to options market experts, and stock and options quotation services. The more extensive the level of additional services, the greater the value of a paper-trading site.

THE CASE FOR PAPER TRADING

Why should you paper trade? Of course, using a site with many valuable support features will invariably help everyone, but why not go directly to real-time trading? Even if you agree that paper trading makes sense, why not paper trade on a brokerage site? Because some online services offer modeling features to one degree or another, some might think it makes sense to simply paper trade where they will eventually trade with real money.

Key Point

Using a nonbrokerage paper-trading site is a good form of discipline. It keeps you from the temptation to enter real-money trades before you are ready.

The reasons to paper trade as a first step, apart from a brokerage account, include:

- *Paper trading with a brokerage could be too tempting.* It might seem convenient to open a brokerage account and paper trade for a while, until you are comfortable with a range of options trades. But because real-time trades are also available, it is all too easy to abandon paper trading and go for the money. Without experience in a range of possible outcomes, this could be a costly mistake. It is human nature to fall into a habit of watching the market and seeing opportunities come and go while you paper trade. "If I had only put money into that last week" is a dangerous and self-defeating way of thinking about options. Remember, on the long side you have to fight the odds because three-quarters of all options expire worthless. On the short side, you need to know what you're doing before entering a two-part trade (covered call) or, even more so, a naked position. This is why you should use a paper-trading service that restricts your trades to the same trading level you will experience when you begin trading for real. When you open your brokerage account, you are asked to fill out and submit an options-trading application, and based on your information and account dollar level, the brokerage firm will limit your trading. First-time traders will be allowed to open long positions only, or to write covered calls; more advanced strategies won't be allowed. To get experience in these advanced ideas, paper trading will be your only initial outlet.

Key Point

An options-trading application is a brokerage firm's way to ensure that anyone trading options has been screened in advance.

- *Using real money before you have experienced the outcome of a trade is risky.* Many people begin studying options by reading books or observing the market. But a theory about how a trade will work out is not the same as putting real money at risk. A lot of first-time options traders focus on exotic, complicated, and high-risk trades, so that experience comes at a price, usually meaning losing money. With paper trading, you can try the most exotic, high-risk strategies you want without actually risking any loss. While you should approach paper trading seriously, it does provide you with a risk-free method for finding out the true risk level of a particular strategy.

Key Point

Many options strategies look good on paper. But when you execute a trade, the experience might be far different than you expected. This is why paper trading is a sensible starting point.

- *Once you start trading for real, especially using a discount brokerage service, you have little or no support.* The advantage of discount services is that trades are executed for very little cost. In fact, the combined cost of opening and closing an option position is usually under a quarter point ($25), sometimes less. This also assumes you trade a single contract. Trading multiple contracts lowers the per-option cost even more. But this savings also comes without any advice or guidance, so you have to find your own way. Options traders, of course, should be able to execute their own trades and also to make their own decisions without help. But everyone needs to start somewhere, and paper trading is an excellent way to begin. Think of paper trading as learning to ride a bike. The training wheels are useful and they help avoid serious injury. At some point, the training wheels have to come off, but not until you are ready.

Key Point

Some investors depend on the safety net of a commission-based broker. But options investors should be prepared to proceed on their own. Paper trading helps you gain experience in trading without the risk and without the advice many investors are accustomed to having available.

- The mechanics of options trading take some getting used to. The very fact that options expire makes them much different from the buy-and-hold strategy of stocks. Many aspects associated with options trading, including margin requirements and limitations, matching of risk with financial resources, and even the details of placing trades properly, all require a degree of practice. For example, many first-time options traders make the expensive mistake of entering a buy instead of a sell, or vice versa. Paper trading helps you to master the oddities of the market by trying out even advanced trades in a simulated environment.

There are three types of websites offering paper trading:

1. *Free paper trading on sites selling other products.* A site that offers more than mere paper trading is valuable because it lends support to your trading activity, especially if good learning tools are included. Some sites offering paper trading also promote products they are selling. There is nothing wrong with selling products online and, in fact, many marketing sites view free services like paper trading, quotations, and articles as good inducements for traders to visit.

2. *Subscription sites for options traders.* Other sites specialize in paper trading but also offer valuable services as a specific options-related educational service. Many options traders will be willing to pay for paper-trading services because the value in these added services is worth the money.

3. *Options sites providing paper trading and many other services.* A third type of site offers paper trading as well as many other support services, tutorials and articles, and links to education. Because such a site (see the CBOE in the next section) is aimed specifically at options trading, it is informative and full of valuable resources.

TWO SITES WORTH CHECKING

Following are two sites worth checking out. They offer an array of different services, levels of use, and conveniences. Each site should be visited in order to see exactly what is offered and whether it will work for you.

www.investopedia.com

This is a multiresource site that offers an easy-to-use dictionary, articles and tutorials, professional exam preparation, reports, quotes, and financial calculators—as well as free paper trading.

From the home page, go to the link for "simulator" and enter the "Investopedia games" area. Choose the game that includes both stock and options trading. By participating in a game, you are ranked according to the profitability of stock and options trades you enter. This makes paper trading interesting, because it enables you to compete against other investors.

The stock simulator starts you out with a mock portfolio valued at $100,000. This is a nice, tidy sum to begin your portfolio. However, for most individuals, starting out with such a large amount of capital is not realistic. One frustrating aspect of getting into options trading is that for most people, the limitations of capital prevent extensive trading activity. So in that respect, paper trading with a $100,000 portfolio does not approximate a real-world environment for the majority of people.

The system also requires a form of diversification. No one position can exceed 50 percent of your total portfolio value, so that you have to put the cash to work in two or more different stocks and/or option positions.

www.cboe.com

The Chicago Board Options Exchange (CBOE) is the site where options are traded and cleared. Located in Chicago, the exchange is an interesting one, and its website offers an array of tools and features specifically aimed at options traders.

From the home page, link to " tools" and then to "virtual trade." One of the most interesting features of the free CBOE paper-trading page is that it asks you to set up your own trading level. It sets this based on your experience, interests, and skill levels. So as long as you set up the account to honestly reflect your personal experience and knowledge, the site will impose the same restrictions on you as those of a real brokerage firm.

You can also set up the dollar amount of your portfolio from $5,000 and up. You should establish your account to start out at the level you are likely to start in a real trading account, so that your paper-trading experience will take place in an environment similar to the one you'll experience later on, using actual cash.

The CBOE also offers extensive and easy-to-use options quotes. If you do not yet have a brokerage account, this feature is very valuable. Many financial websites offering free quotes are limited to stocks and are not set up for ease of use in options trading. The CBOE is an exception. Its options listings are accessible by linking to "quotes" and then to "delayed option chains." The delayed chain link is practical for most people. It lists all calls and puts on a specified stock on a single page. This feature is valuable because you don't need to know the symbol for an option in advance, a problem many options traders have to struggle with. Quote symbols used to be simple, but after the introduction of long-term equity anticipation security *(LEAPS)* options, they became quite complex. So the CBOE system is just as convenient as most brokerage listing systems.

PROCEEDING WITH A PAPER-TRADING PLAN

To get started in paper trading for options, you may want to take three steps at the same time:

1. *Open a brokerage account or continue with the account you already have.* If you have an existing brokerage account where you trade stocks, continue that activity while you follow the next two steps. If you have not yet begun to trade on any level, open a free brokerage account after researching the terms and trading costs of several brokerage firms.

2. *Complete an options-trading application with your brokerage firm.* Download or request an options-trading application. This form asks you to specify the number of trades you execute per year and your level of experience in options trading. If you are a novice, you will be assigned a low level and probably be allowed only to open long call or put positions, at least as a start. But once you have gained some experience, you can apply to be upgraded to the next level.

3. *Find a paper-trading site that fits your needs and begin actively trading options.* Check out several paper-trading sites and find one that is flexible enough for the kind of trading you want to try. Also, make sure it works. You can open a free account on several sites and navigate your way through the paper-trading feature before deciding whether to remain with a site. Try to think of your paper trades as real; avoid the problem of not taking the paper-trading activity seriously. Begin with a specific portfolio amount and see what kind of net returns you realize through paper trading. That is the only way to ensure that once you begin putting actual money into trades, you will know what to expect.

CALCULATING THE RETURN:
A COMPLEX ASPECT
TO OPTIONS

*A criminal is a person with predatory instincts who
has not sufficient capital to form a corporation.*
　　　　　　　—Howard Scott, *The New Dictionary of Thought*, 1957

The return calculations on your options trades can be complicated. When
you consider the various elements, including your basis and profit in
stock, dividends you earn, and the time your stock and option positions
remain open, this is no easy matter.

In Chapter 2, you found a useful summary for calculating return
on various option positions. In this chapter, these same concepts are
expanded on and developed. There are several potential methods for
return calculations, and the most important points to remember are:
the method you pick has to be realistic, and annualization is a means
for comparing similar risks, not to establish likely returns from options
trades.

FINDING A REALISTIC METHOD

Among the many methods available to you, some are exceptionally complex and involve theoretical valuation. The small increments of difference in these incremental returns versus the easier, faster, and more logical methods make them impractical. The options market is fast moving, and traders have to make decisions in the moment and based on return calculations and risk that are readily comprehended. Some of the methods used by academics do not have practical applications in the real world of options trading.

Key Point

You can expand return and valuation calculations infinitely, but the more obscure the method, the less practical it becomes. It is useful to know about complex methods for valuation of options, but in the real world of trading, you will most likely prefer a simple method over a complex one.

Two of the best-known modeling calculations are worth a brief explanation. The *Black-Scholes model* is named for Fischer Black and Myron Scholes, who together published a scholarly paper in 1973 explaining their theory. The calculation is beyond the scope of this book; however, it is designed to take into account the elements of time value, stock price variation, an assumed market rate of interest, and time remaining until expiration. The formula sets a fair price for options, and several variations of the original formula have evolved since 1973.[1]

One problem with the original Black-Scholes model is that it was based on European-style option expiration. Under the European rule, options can be exercised only immediately before expiration and not whenever the owner wants, as is the case with American-style options.

Key Point

Black-Scholes is a well-known model, but it is based on assumptions about interest rates and fixed expiration. Even with its variations, this model is too obscure for most applications.

---

[1] *Fischer Black and Myron Scholes, "The Pricing of Options and Corporate Liabilities," Journal of Political Economy 81, no. 3 (1973): 637–654.*

An alternative calculation is known as the *binomial model.* This calculation was developed in 1979 and allows for possible exercise at different moments in an option's life. These times are selected between the current date and expiration to demonstrate how time valuation adjustment would be made. One major flaw in the binomial model, however, is that it assumes the stock's price is always reasonable; in other words, this model succeeds only if you also accept the premise of *the efficient market.* Clearly, in the volatile and emotional market environment, highly volatile stocks will not behave in an efficient manner, so that the binomial model is just that—a model. It is instructive, however, because it also assumes a risk-neutral posture in valuation of the underlying stock. If such efficiency worked in the real world, option valuation, risk analysis, and return calculations would be quite simple.[2]

Neither the Black-Scholes nor the binomial model will be able to

Valuable Resource
You can use a calculator to see how the Black-Scholes model works out, requiring only that you enter your assumptions into the model. See www.blackscholes.net/.

provide a practical, realistic method for determining option values. However, in reviewing options for any trade you have in mind, the apparent value of an option at any time is best made in comparisons between other options on the same stock. You will consider time until expiration, the level of intrinsic versus time value, proximity between a stock's current value and the option's striking price, and then dollar value of the option itself. This process applies whether you are considering long or short positions; using calls, puts, or combinations of both; and willing to take high risks or only very conservative risks. The process is the same in any case.

In evaluating risk, you will also want to make a judgment call about the level of exposure versus the premium value of an option. For example, you might not be willing to enter a covered call for only $200 over the next two months. However, if the stock's current market value is $20,

[2] J. C. Cox, S. A. Ross, and M. Rubinstein, "Options Pricing: A Simplified Approach," *Journal of Financial Economics 7* (1979): 229–263.

that is a 10 percent return (60 percent annualized). If the stock is worth $60, the same option yields only 3.33 percent (20 percent annualized). All the elements have to be brought into the decision, including the yield itself, dollar value of the option, time to expiration, and your risk profile.

Key Point

The binomial model would be excellent if the efficient market theory were realistic. But as anyone who has tracked the market knows, it is far from efficient.

ANNUALIZING MODELS AND GUIDELINES

Annualize returns, not to establish a realistic expectation for outcomes on similar transactions, or to set goals for yourself, but to ensure consistency in comparisons. A discussion of annualization beyond the obvious technique is worthwhile. The basic concept is easily comprehended: If you have two option profits, both at 10 percent, they are not necessarily equal. One held for six months will annualize at 20 percent; another held for 24 months annualizes at only 5 percent. So rather than attempting to compare two options with 10 percent returns, annualization enables you to make a valid time-based comparison. Clearly, developing a 10 percent profit in six months is far better because (in theory) you can create and duplicate the same outcome four times over a two-year period.

Key Point

Annualizing stock-based returns is a smart way to ensure like-kind comparisons. The same principle does not apply to options returns, so annualizing does not provide you with a realistic expectation of future outcomes.

This preliminary view of annualization is completely valid when comparing compound interest in savings accounts, money market funds, or certificates of deposit (or in calculating annual percentage rates on a home mortgage). The time value of money is fairly straightforward for most calculations of the *time value of money*, which is what annualization is all about. But when it comes to option return calculations, annualization can distort outcomes and even build unrealistic expectations.

time value of money

The concept observing that earnings potential adds value to a sum of money. As long as money is put to use earning profit, the present discounted value of the future fund relies on (1) the interest rate, (2) compounding method, and (3) time involved until the final result can be achieved.

Valuable Resource

A comprehensive explanation of time value of money and its various uses is found at the financial dictionary: http://financial-dictionary.thefreedictionary.com/ Time+Value+of+Money.

For example, a sum of $100 invested in a savings account at 3 percent simple annual interest would grow to $103 in one year. A similar investment in stock may grow to $103 in months and, upon sale, earn the same amount but in half the time. Thus, looking back and comparing these two outcomes, the time value of money invested in that particular stock was twice that of the money left in the savings account.

Time value of money does not take into account varying degrees of risk, and this is where annualization is flawed regarding options. For example, you might take substantial risks in buying a long call for 3 ($300) and seeing it grow to a net of $400 in one month, and achieve exactly the same return writing a covered call and realizing a $100 profit in three months. While the first example annualizes at 400 percent, the second annualizes at only 133 percent. But the risk levels are substantially different, so annualizing does not make these outcomes truly comparative.

Key Point

An annualized return can be comparative only when risks are also comparative. As a consequence, you cannot depend on annualized returns for dissimilar positions and expect to gain any reliable conclusions from the analysis.

You achieve a comparative annualized return only when you compare two transactions that are substantially the same, but for different options and stocks and over different time periods. For example, comparing any two long option positions (between calls, puts, or a mix with a call in one case and a put in another) is a substantially identical type of option transaction. The fact that the risk levels are essentially similar lends itself to the use of annualization as a useful device for ensuring that your comparisons are accurate.

You might vary long risks by selecting different timing until expiration, in-the-money versus out-of-the-money positions, or even proximity between striking price and market value of the underlying stock. But the point remains valid: Annualization with options is useful in comparing similar risks. It is not a reliable means for comparing dissimilar risk positions.

Because many option positions are exceptionally short-term, it is also not realistic to point to a 400 percent annualized return (or even a 133 percent return) and call it typical. Many options promoters have pointed to such examples to sell seminar "get rich" programs, but that level of outcome is not going to repeat consistently. So another caveat about annualizing is that it should not be viewed as an approximation of returns you can reasonably expect to realize on typical transactions. It is useful as a means of return comparisons only when risk attributes are the same between the transactions annualized.

AN OVERVIEW OF BASIC CALCULATION FOR CALLS

On a realistic level, your calculations of returns on option trades should be possible with a desk calculator; it should be quick and easy, and the results should tell you all that you need to know immediately.

For all long positions, the basic calculations are very straightforward. To review, various terms are used to describe an outcome, including *return on investment, yield,* and numerous others. The expression *net return* is useful because it is simple, but it qualifies the return. By *net,* this expression means actual dollar values realized and expressed as a percentage. So transaction costs are deducted from both the buy and sell sides of the transaction, and the return is calculated based on dollars-in and dollars-out results, or the "net."

Example

The Safety Net: You purchase a call for 0.75 ($75) and also pay a brokerage fee of $12.50. Your basis in the long position is $87.50. Two months later, you sell for 1.5 ($150). Your brokerage firm deducts another $12.50 from proceeds and credits your account with $137.50. To calculate net return, first calculate the net profit:

$137.50 - $87.50 = $50.00

Next, divide the net profit by the original net basis:

$50.00/$137.50 = 36.4%

If you also want to annualize this return (to compare it to other long positions), you divide the percentage by the holding period (2 months) and multiply by 12 months:

36.4%/2 x 12 = 218.4%

As with all other instances of annualizing returns, this should not be used to set a standard for outcomes in future long positions. It is useful only for comparisons between similar risk levels of trades.

Valuable Resource
The CBOE provides a free option calculator. Check it out at www.cboe.com/LearnCenter/OptionCalculator.aspx.

The long position calculation is simple compared to calculations for short positions. In the short position, you sell first and realize a profit when one of three events occurs: (1) the position is closed when you enter a buy; (2) the option is exercised; or (3) the option expires worthless.

Key Point
Calculating net return for long positions is simple because the levels of risk, capital requirements, and outcomes are well understood. The same argument is not true for short-position net returns.

Short-position calculations for calls are complicated by three factors:

1. Different levels of capital have to be kept in your brokerage account for uncovered calls or puts.
2. When you write covered calls, you have to consider your basis in the stock as part of your capital at risk.
3. If a covered call is exercised, you have to consider gain on the option *and* gain or loss on the stock, and decide whether to include dividends in your net return.

If you own stock and sell covered calls, you can perform one type of net return calculation separate and apart from the value or profit on stock. Assuming your purpose in selling the calls is to increase current income and not to force exercise, you may consider only call premium and calculate the return in one of four ways:

1. *You close the position and calculate option-based net return.* When you close a covered call, either to take a profit or to avoid or defer exercise, you can calculate net return in the same way you do for trading long options. The difference between sell and buy is divided by the net buy price, and the resulting percentage is your preannualized net profit or loss.

Example

Upside-Down Return: You sold a covered call four months ago and received a premium of 5 ($500). Net proceeds came to $487.50. Last week, you entered a buy to close order at 2 ($200). Net cost was $212.50. Your net return considering only the option transaction was $275 ($487.50–$212.50). That was 129.4 percent based on the closing buy price. This is a somewhat unrealistic form of return, because the transaction occurs in reverse. You cannot, however, calculate the return based on the initial sales price of the option. This format may be useful for comparative purposes, but it does not give you a full view of how net return worked in this example.

2. *You close the position and calculate net return based on the entire position.* A different point of view for covered call returns will be based on outcome for the whole position, including option premium, capital gain or loss on the stock, and dividend income during the holding period. The calculation includes everything, and there is a justification for performing the calculation in this manner: Your selection of one striking price over another affects the outcome in case of exercise. Consider the difference between making a 2-point capital *gain* or accepting a 3-point capital *loss*. This comparison is valid if you choose between two striking prices when current value of the stock resides in between.

Examples

A Striking Proposal: You may base potential profit or loss on the striking price of the option, regardless of your actual basis in the stock. You own 100 shares of stock you originally purchased at $32 per share. Today, the stock's value is at $42.50. You want to write a covered call and you have reviewed both 40 and 45 striking prices. The 40 call provides higher premium, but the 45 is also attractive and out of the money. So you calculate the total net return including dividends you will earn between now and expiration date; capital gain or loss (based on current value rather than original price), and the option premium.

Your Basic Basis: Given the same facts as in the previous example, you may consider striking prices of 40 and 45, given the current value of stock at $42.50. However, in making the comparison, you use your original cost per share of $32. This enables you to judge the relative value of one option over the other in deciding whether to write the covered call.

Both situations are somewhat distorted because option profit or loss is combined with the stock capital gain. However, net returns aside, it is clear that the comparison has to be made in order to judge the viability of one striking price over the other.

3. *The covered call is exercised and you calculate option and stock profits separately.* The solution to the dilemma of mixing option, stock, and dividend sources of net return is to perform analysis separately. You use the stock basis to consider whether you actually want to create one level of profit or another. But when it comes to judging the results, you separate the stock and option profits.

Example

Separate but Equal: You are considering writing a covered call on stock you originally bought at $28 per share. Today, you can write calls with striking prices of 25 or 30, and both are attractively priced. However, in a separate analysis of each, you abandon the 25 striking price because, if exercised, that would create a capital loss in the stock of 3 points. The 25 call is available for 4.50 today. The combined income from stock and option would only be $150, whereas exercise of the 30 call would include 3 points of capital gain in the stock plus 2 points in the option. You calculate the potential profit or loss separately, but you use the comparison to eliminate the in-the-money call.

return on capital employed (ROCE)

In stock and options trading, net return based on cash left on deposit in a margin account, to include all forms of net return minus transaction costs and interest charged on the balance financed; leveraged return combining minimum margin requirements with borrowed funds.

4. *Any covered call outcome is computed strictly on the basis of capital on deposit.* Yet another method for calculating option profits is based on the use of margin rather than actual basis in either stock or option. This *return on capital employed* (ROCE) is a cash-for-cash calculation when applied to options trading. Those investing solely in stocks often use this leveraged approach to analysis. For example, if you buy stock at $50 per share, you are required to have only $2,500 in your account, and the rest is loaned to you by your brokerage firm. The calculation of net return has to include the interest charged during your holding period, but the return is potentially higher because you have less cash committed to the position. If you net a 5-point gain, that is 10 percent based on the stock's growth in value (from $50 to $55 per share). But if you have only $2,500 at risk, a 5-point gain is 20 percent net return (assuming the return is net of interest expense).

The same approach can be used when you buy or sell options or when you write covered calls. You might have only half the stock's value on deposit with the balance on margin; you may also be required to leave only a portion of an option's value in your account in order to open an option position. The calculation of net return in this case is not going to be based on the movement of a number of points, but rather on the change in your actual cash position. It requires that you add together the stock capital gains, option profits, and dividend income, and deduct any losses as well as transaction fees and interest charged by your brokerage firm. The net income is not based on the prices of stock and option but on the amount of cash you had on deposit.

Key Point

When you base net return calculations on cash actually at risk, you have two variables. First is the higher risk of trading on margin, and second is the greater potential gained from leverage. These are two aspects of the same advantage/problem.

The leveraged approach will produce much higher percentage gains, but it also involves greater risk. When you suffer net losses, you will be required to make up the difference in cash. For example, if you have $2,500 at risk on a $50 stock and it falls 5 points (10 percent), you will lose $500, or 20 percent of your cash on deposit. The same doubling effect applies to options. For example, if you deposit $200 to buy an option priced at 4 ($400) and it expires worthless, you not only lose your $200 on deposit, you also have to pay your brokerage firm another $200 plus transaction fees and interest. In that example, your net loss will exceed 100 percent.

ANTICIPATING THE LIKELY RETURN

Calculating potential profit or loss on a variety of trades demonstrates that you often operate on thin margins. The judgment call as to whether a particular strategy will or will not be profitable is often based on consideration of a single option contract. In practice, you can cut your transaction costs considerably by using multiple contracts. This also expands your potential secondary strategies.

You should not decide to use multiple contracts solely to reduce your costs, but that is one way to amend your calculation of profitability for a particular strategy. The use of multiple contracts also opens up the potential for advanced strategies and altering them, spreading or reducing risks, and creating a range of profitable outcome while better managing the chances of risk.

In evaluating strategies, you will also benefit by calculating the *expected return*. This is the probability of several different outcomes, averaged to create a "most likely" outcome, and this is useful in determining whether a particular strategy is worth the risk.

expected return

The likely return from an option strategy, based on analysis of a range of possible outcomes, used to identify the most reasonable return a trader should expect to realize.

Key Point

Return calculations are rather inflexible when based on single contracts. While examples using only one option clarify possible outcomes, in practice you have much greater flexibility and lower trading costs by trading in multiple contract increments.

Example

Great Expectations: You are considering writing a covered call on stock you own. The stock recently rallied so you see a covered call as a way of taking profits in the event the stock falls. If the covered call is exercised, you are also willing to sell your stock at the striking price. You can receive 5 ($500) for a call expiring in three months that is today at the money. Because you expect the stock's price to retreat, this seems like a good plan. Expected return is based on a series of several possible outcomes:

- The stock will continue to rise and the call will be exercised. You think there is a 25 percent chance that this will happen. In this case, your overall profit (including only call premium) would be 100 percent.
- The stock will remain close to the striking price of the option but will not go in the money. You would wait for the option to lose half its value and then buy to close and take the net profit. For this, you believe there is only a 10 percent chance. Your profit in this case would be 50 percent (based only on the call's premium).
- The stock will retreat back to previous trading levels and remain there, in which case you expect the option's premium to retreat to 2.5 or less. In that case, you would probably close the position and take your profit. This would also create a 50 percent profit. You believe there is a 40 percent chance this will occur.
- The stock will retreat below previous trading levels and the option premium will fall drastically. In this outcome, you would be inclined to let the call expire worthless. This would create a 100 percent profit. You believe there is a 25 percent chance that this will happen.

Given these possible outcomes, expected return would consist of calculating the likely range of outcomes:

Striking Price	Return	Expectation	Result
A	100%	25%	25%
B	50	10	5
C	40	40	16
D	100	25	25
Total		100%	71%

The expected return in this case is 71 percent. This is also based on the recognition of covered call writing as having good profit potential, but this example is limited to analysis of the option premium. It does not take into account the risks involving the stock. You may also want to think about the possibilities of the stock's rising far above the striking price (meaning the covered call strategy involves a lost opportunity) *or* falls below. That means that, if the stock's price were to retreat and remain lower, you would have lost the chance to sell at a profit when the price per share had been higher. So expected return might be further extended to include an evaluation of outcomes based on stock profit or loss as well. Exercise of a covered call at a striking price above original basis is invariably profitable. But a paper loss is a risk to consider, just as lost opportunity in the event of exercise.

Key Point

Expected return is useful for identifying a range of likely outcomes. In situations where expected return is minimal given the range of risk, this calculation can be used to decide to not proceed.

You can take analysis of this type to any extent you desire. But at some point, options traders need to make decisions and not spend excessive time on highly detailed theories about likely outcomes. Hopefully, before investing in any options positions, you will appreciate the range of risks as well as the potential profit or loss. But most options traders soon discover that they can take analysis only so far; eventually, they need to act, and often decisions have to be made quickly to take advantage of ever-changing price conditions.

Every options trader needs to calculate a practical and accurate outcome to the potential trades involved. Everything works out well on paper, of course; but when you consider the cost of transactions, interest on margin balances, and income taxes, you quickly realize that these are elements of risk. No one can predict every possible outcome; but you can improve your percentages in all forms of options trading by identifying and performing reliable forms of likely returns. The calculations do not need to be complicated, but they do need to be consistent and accurate.

THE END

GLOSSARY

How often misused words generate misleading thoughts.
—Herbert Spencer, *Principles of Ethics*, 1892–1893

after-tax breakeven point
The point level at which you will break even on an option trade, considering the taxes due on capital gains you will be required to pay for trading options.

annualized basis
A method for comparing rates of return for holdings of varying periods, in which all returns are expressed as though investments had been held over a full year. It involves dividing the rate of return by the number of months the positions were open, and multiplying the result by 12.

approval level
A brokerage house's limitation on types of options strategies customers are allowed to enter, based on experience, knowledge, and account value.

assignment
The act of exercise against a seller, done on a random basis or in accordance with orderly procedures developed by the Options Clearing Corporation and brokerage firms.

at the money
The status of an option when the underlying stock's value is identical to the option's striking price.

auction market
The public exchanges in which stocks, bonds, options, and other products are traded publicly, and in which values are established by ever-changing supply and demand on the part of buyers and sellers.

automatic exercise
Action taken by the Options Clearing Corporation at the time of expiration, when an in-the-money option has not been otherwise exercised or canceled.

average down

A strategy involving the purchase of stock when its market value is decreasing. The average cost of shares bought in this manner is consistently higher than current market value, so a portion of the paper loss on declining stock value is absorbed, enabling covered call writers to sell calls and profit even when the stock's market value has declined.

average up

A strategy involving the purchase of stock when its market value is increasing. The average cost of shares bought in this manner is consistently lower than current market value, enabling covered call writers to sell calls in the money when the basis is below the striking price.

beta

A measurement of relative volatility of a stock, made by comparing the degree of price movement to that of a larger index of stock prices.

binomial model

An option valuation formula developed in 1979, based on selection of various times between valuation date and expiration. The formula is risk neutral but also assumes that the efficient market theory applies in all cases.

Black-Scholes model

A formula used to estimate a fair price for an option contract, originated in 1973. The calculation takes into account the elements of time value, stock price variation, an assumed market interest rate, and the time left until expiration.

book value

The actual value of a company, more accurately called *book value per share*; the value of a company's capital (assets less liabilities), divided by the number of outstanding shares of stock.

breakeven price

Also called the *breakeven point*. The price of the underlying stock at which the option investor breaks even. For call buyers, this price is the number of points above striking price equal to the call premium cost; for put buyers, this price is the number of points below striking price equal to the put premium cost.

breakout

The movement of a stock's price below support level or above resistance level.

buyer
An investor who purchases a call or a put option; the buyer realizes a profit if the value of stock moves above the specified price (call) or below the specified price (put).

call
An option acquired by a buyer or granted by a seller to buy 100 shares of stock at a fixed price within a specified time period.

called away
The result of having stock assigned. Upon exercise, 100 shares of the seller's stock are called away at the striking price.

chartist
An analyst who studies charts of a stock's price movement in the belief that recent patterns can be used to predict upcoming price changes and directions.

class
All options traded on a single underlying stock, including different striking prices and expiration dates.

closed position
The status of a position when an initial opening transaction has been offset and the position is no longer open.

closing purchase transaction
A transaction to close a short position, executed by buying an option previously sold, canceling it out.

closing sale transaction
A transaction to close a long position, executed by selling an option previously bought, closing it out.

contingent purchase
A strategy involving the sale of a put and willingness to accept exercise, which will result in purchasing 100 shares of stock. The strategy makes sense when the individual believes the striking price is a reasonable price for the stock.

contract
A single option, the agreement providing the buyer with the terms that option grants. Those terms include identification of the stock, the cost of the option, the date the option will expire, and the fixed price per share of the stock to be bought or sold under the rights of the option.

conversion
The process of moving assigned stock from the seller of a call option or to the seller of a put option.

core earnings
As defined by Standard & Poor's, the after-tax earnings generated from a corporation's principal business.

cover
The ownership of 100 shares of the underlying stock for each call sold, providing sellers the ability to deliver shares already held, in the event of exercise.

covered call
A call sold to create an open short position, when the seller also owns 100 shares of stock for each call sold.

current market value
The market value of a stock at any given time.

cycle
The pattern of expiration dates of options for a particular underlying stock. The three cycles occur in four-month intervals and are described by month abbreviations. They are (1) January, April, July, and October, or JAJO; (2) February, May, August, and November, or FMAN; and (3) March, June, September, and December, or MJSD.

debt investment
An investment in the form of a loan made to earn interest, such as the purchase of a bond.

debt ratio
A ratio used to follow trends in debt capitalization. To compute, divide long-term debt by total capitalization; the result is expressed as a percentage.

deep in
The condition when the underlying stock's current market value is 5 points or more above the striking price of the call or below the striking price of the put.

deep out
The condition when the underlying stock's current market value is 5 points or more below the striking price of the call or above the striking price of the put.

delivery
The movement of stock ownership from one owner to another. In the case of exercised options, shares are registered to the new owner on receipt of payment.

delta
The degree of change in option premium in relation to changes in the underlying stock. If the call option's degree of change exceeds the change in the underlying stock, it is called an *up delta*; when the change is less than in the underlying stock, it is called a *down delta*. The reverse terminology is applied to puts.

discount
The reduction in the basis of stock, equal to the amount of option premium received. A benefit in selling covered calls, the discount provides downside protection and protects long positions.

dividend yield
Dividends paid per share of common stock, expressed as a percentage computed by dividing dividend paid per share by the current market value of the stock.

dollar cost averaging
A strategy for investing over time, either buying a fixed number of shares or investing a fixed dollar amount, in regular intervals. The result is an averaging of overall price. If market value increases, average cost is always lower than current market value; if market value decreases, average cost is always higher than current market value.

downside protection
A strategy involving the purchase of one put for every 100 shares of the underlying stock that you own. This insures you against losses to some degree. For every in-the-money point the stock falls, the put will increase in value by one point. Before exercise, you may sell the put and take a profit, offsetting stock losses, or exercise the put and sell the shares at the striking price.

Dow Theory
A theory that market trends are predictable based on changes in market averages.

early exercise
The act of exercising an option prior to expiration date.

earnings per share

A commonly used method for reporting profits. Net profits for a year or for the latest quarter are divided by the number of shares of common stock outstanding as of the ending date of the financial report. The result is expressed as a dollar value.

EBITDA

A popular measurement of cash flow, an acronym for earnings before interest, taxes, depreciation, and amortization.

efficient market hypothesis

A theory stating that current stock prices reflect all information publicly known about a company.

equity investment

An investment in the form of part ownership, such as the purchase of shares of stock in a corporation.

exercise

The act of buying stock under the terms of the call option or selling stock under the terms of the put option, at the price per share specified in the option contract.

expiration date

The date on which an option becomes worthless, which is specified in the option contract.

expiration time

The latest possible time to place an order for cancellation or exercise of an option, which may vary depending on the brokerage firm executing the order and on the option itself.

expected return

The likely return from an option strategy, based on analysis of a range of possible outcomes, used to identify the most reasonable return a trader should expect to realize.

extrinsic value

The portion of an option's premium generated from volatility in the underlying stock and from market perception of potential price changes until expiration date; a non-intrinsic portion of the premium value not specifically caused by the element of time.

fundamental analysis

A study of financial information and attributes of a company's management and competitive position, as a means for selecting stocks.

gamma
A measurement of the speed of change in delta, relative to price movement in the underlying stock.

Greeks
A series of analytical tests of option risk and volatility, so called because they are named for letters of the Greek alphabet.

hedge ratio
Alternate name for the delta, the measurement of changes in option value relative to changes in stock value.

incremental return
A technique for avoiding exercise while increasing profits with written calls. When the value of the underlying stock rises, a single call is closed at a loss and replaced with two or more call writes with later expiration dates, producing cash and a net profit in the exchange.

in the money
The status of a call option when the underlying stock's market value is higher than the option's striking price, or of a put option when the underlying stock's market value is lower than the option's striking price.

intrinsic value
That portion of an option's current value equal to the number of points that it is in the money. One point equals one dollar of value per share; so 35 points equals $35 per share.

know your customer
A rule requiring brokers to be aware of the risk, knowledge level, and capital profile of each client, designed to ensure that recommendations are suitable for each individual.

last trading day
The Friday preceding the third Saturday of the expiration month of an option.

LEAPS
Long-term equity anticipation security, long-term option contracts that work just like standardized options, but with expiration up to three years.

leverage
The use of investment capital in a way that a relatively small amount of money enables the investor to control a relatively large value. This is achieved through borrowing—for example, using

borrowed money to purchase stocks or bonds—or through the purchase of options, which exist for only a short period of time but enable the option buyer to control 100 shares of stock. As a general rule, the use of leverage increases potential for profit as well as for loss.

liquid market
A market in which buyers and sellers are matched to one another, and the exchange absorbs any imbalances between the two sides.

listed option
An option traded on a public exchange and listed in the published reports in the financial press.

lock in
To freeze the price of the underlying stock by selling a covered call. As long as the call position is open, the writer is locked into the striking price, regardless of current market value of the stock. In the event of exercise, the stock is delivered at the locked-in price.

long position
The status assumed by investors when they enter a buy order in advance of entering a sell order. The long position is closed by later entering a sell order, or through expiration.

loss zone
The price range of the underlying stock in which the option investor loses. A limited loss exists for option buyers, since the premium cost is the maximum loss that can be realized.

lost opportunity risk (stock)
The risk stockholders experience in tying up capital over the long term, causing lost opportunities that could be taken if capital were available.

margin
An account with a brokerage firm containing a minimum level of cash and securities to provide collateral for short positions or for purchases for which payment has not yet been made.

margin requirement
The maximum amount of outstanding risk investors are allowed to hold in their portfolio, or the maximum unfunded dollar level allowed when trading on margin.

market value
The value of an investment at any given time or date; the amount a buyer is willing to pay to acquire an investment and what a seller is also willing to receive to transfer the same investment.

married put

The status of a put used to hedge a long position. Each put owned protects 100 shares of the underlying stock held in the portfolio. If the stock declines in value, the put's value will increase and offset the loss.

multiple

The P/E's outcome, the number of times current price per share is above annual earnings per share; for example, if the P/E is 10, then current price per share is 10 times higher than the latest reported earnings per share.

naked option

An option sold in an opening sale transaction when the seller (writer) does not own 100 shares of the underlying stock.

naked position

Status for investors when they assume short positions in calls without also owning 100 shares of the underlying stock for each call written.

net basis

The cost of stock when reduced by premium received for selling covered calls; the true net cost of stock after discounting original cost.

net return

The percentage return on an investment, based on dollar amounts going in and coming out, after transaction fees.

odd lot

A lot of shares that contains fewer than the more typical *round lot* trading unit of 100 shares.

opening purchase transaction

An initial transaction to buy, also known as the action of *going long*.

opening sale transaction

An initial transaction to sell, also known as the action of *going short*.

open interest

The number of open contracts of a particular option at any given time, which can be used to measure market interest.

open position
The status of a trade when a purchase (a long position) or a sale (a short position) has been made, and before cancellation, exercise, or expiration.

option
The right to buy or to sell 100 shares of stock at a specified, fixed price and by a specified date in the future.

orderly settlement
The smooth process of buying and selling, in full confidence that the terms and conditions of options contracts will be honored in a timely manner.

out of the money
The status of a call option when the underlying stock's market value is lower than the option's striking price, or of a put option when the underlying stock's market value is higher than the option's striking price.

paper profits
Also called *unrealized profits*, values existing only on paper but not taken at the time; paper profits (or paper losses) become realized only if a closing transaction is executed.

paper trading
Online "mock trading" of stocks and options using a hypothetical sum of cash, to test strategies in a realistic environment but without placing real money at risk.

parity
The condition of an option at expiration, when the total premium consists of intrinsic value and no time value.

premium value
The current price of an option, which a buyer pays and a seller receives at the time of the transaction. The amount of premium is expressed as the dollar value of the option, but without dollar signs; for example, stating that an option is "at 3" means its current market value is $300.

price/earnings ratio
A popular indicator used by stock market investors to rate and compare stocks. The current market value of the stock is divided by the most recent earnings per share to arrive at the P/E ratio.

profit margin
The most commonly used measurement of corporate operations, computed by dividing net profits by gross sales.

profit zone
The price range of the underlying stock in which the option investor realizes a profit. For the call buyer, the profit zone extends upward from the breakeven price. For the put buyer, the profit zone extends downward from the breakeven price.

pro forma earnings
"as a matter of form" (Latin); a company's earnings based on estimates or forecasts with hypothetical numbers in place of known or actual revenues, costs, or earnings.

prospectus
A document designed to disclose all the risk characteristics associated with a particular investment.

put
An option acquired by a buyer or granted by a seller to sell 100 shares of stock at a fixed price within a specified time period.

put to seller
The action of exercising a put and requiring the seller to purchase 100 shares of stock at the fixed striking price.

quality of earnings
A measurement of the reliability of financial reports. A high quality of earnings means the report reflects the real and accurate operations of a corporation and may be used reliably to forecast likely future growth trends.

random walk
A theory about market pricing, stating that prices of stocks cannot be predicted because price movement is entirely random.

rate of return
The yield from investing, calculated by dividing net cash profit upon sale by the amount spent at purchase.

ready market

A liquid market, one in which buyers can easily sell their holdings, or in which sellers can easily find buyers, at current market prices.

realized profits

Profits taken at the time a position is closed.

Regulation T

A Federal Reserve Board (FRB) rule defining customer cash account minimum levels based on strategies employed.

relative volatility

The degree of volatility in comparative form, such as between portfolios or between a specific stock and other stocks or markets.

resistance level

The highest trading price, under present conditions, above which the price of the stock is not likely to rise.

return if exercised

The estimated rate of return option sellers will earn in the event the buyer exercises the option. The calculation includes profit or loss in the underlying stock, dividends earned, and premium received for selling the option.

return if unchanged

The estimated rate of return option sellers will earn in the event the buyer does not exercise the option. The calculation includes dividends earned on the underlying stock, and the premium received for selling the option.

return on capital employed (ROCE)

In stock and options trading, net return based on cash left on deposit in a margin account, to include all forms of net return minus transaction costs and interest charged on the balance financed; leveraged return combining minimum margin requirements with borrowed funds.

rho

A calculation of the effect of interest rate trends on option valuation; a long-term analytical tool rather than one of immediate value.

roll-down

The replacement of one written call with another that has a lower striking price.

roll-forward

The replacement of one written call with another with the same striking price, but a later expiration date.

roll-up

The replacement of one written call with another that has a higher striking price.

round lot

A lot of 100 shares of stock or of higher numbers divisible by 100, the usual trading unit on the public exchanges.

sector

A specific segment of the market defined by product or service offered by a company. Factors affecting value (cyclical, economic, or market based) make each sector distinct and different from other sectors, also affecting option valuation.

seller

An investor who grants a right in an option to someone else; the seller realizes a profit if the value of the stock moves below the specified price (call) or above the specified price (put).

sensitivity

The degree of change in an option's value based solely on the time remaining until expiration.

series

A group of options sharing identical terms.

settlement date

The date on which a buyer is required to pay for purchases, or on which a seller is entitled to receive payment. For stocks, settlement date is three business days after the transaction. For options, settlement date is one business day from the date of the transaction.

share

A unit of ownership in the capital of a corporation.

short position

The status assumed by investors when they enter a sale order in advance of entering a buy order. The short position is closed by later entering a buy order, or through expiration.

short selling

A strategy in the stock market in which shares of stock are first sold, creating a short position for the investor, and later bought in a closing purchase transaction.

speculation
The use of money to assume risks for short-term profit, in the knowledge that substantial or total losses are one possible outcome. Buying calls for leverage is one form of speculation. The buyer may earn a very large profit in a matter of days, or could lose the entire amount invested.

striking price
The fixed price to be paid for 100 shares of stock, specified in the option contract; the transaction price per share of stock upon exercise of that option, regardless of the current market value of the stock.

suitability
Standard by which a particular investment or market strategy is judged. The investor's knowledge and experience with options represent important suitability standards. Strategies are appropriate only if the investor understands the market and can afford to take the risks involved.

supply and demand
The market forces that determine the current value for stocks. The number of buyers represents demand for shares, and the number of sellers represents supply. The price of stocks rises as demand increases, and falls as supply increases.

support level
The lowest trading price, under present conditions, below which the price of the stock is not likely to fall.

synthetic position
A strategy in which stock and option positions are matched up to protect against unfavorable price movement. When you own stock and also buy a put to protect against downward price movement, it creates a synthetic call. When you are short on stock and buy a call, it creates a synthetic put.

tangible book value per share
The net value of a company, computed by subtracting all liabilities from all assets, and further reducing the net by all intangible assets. The net of tangible assets is then divided by the number of outstanding shares of common stock.

tau
A measurement of an option's premium value in relation to the underlying stock's changes in volatility.

tax put
A strategy combining the sale of stock at a loss—taken for tax purposes—and the sale of a put at the same time. The premium received on the put offsets the stock loss; if the put is exercised, the stock is purchased at the striking price.

technical analysis
A study of trends and patterns of price movement in stocks, including price per share, the shape of price movements on charts, high and low ranges, and trends in pricing over time.

terms
Also called *standardized terms*, the attributes that describe an option, including the striking price, expiration month, type of option (call or put), and the underlying stock.

theta
A measurement of an option's value based on time until expiration.

time value of money
The concept observing that earnings potential adds value to a sum of money. As long as money is put to use earning profit, the present discounted value of the future fund relies on (1) the interest rate, (2) compounding method, and (3) time involved until the final result can be achieved.

time value
That portion of an option's current premium above intrinsic value.

total capitalization
The combination of long-term debt (debt capital) and stockholders' equity (equity capital), which in combination represents the financing of corporate operations and long-term growth.

total return
The combined return including income from selling a call, capital gain from profit on selling the stock, and dividends earned and received. Total return may be calculated in two ways: return if the option is exercised, and return if the option expires worthless.

trading range
The price range between support and resistance; the current price area where stock purchase and sale levels occur.

uncovered option

The same as a naked option—the sale of an option not covered, or protected, by the ownership of 100 shares of the underlying stock.

underlying stock

The stock on which the option grants the right to buy or sell, which is specified in every option contract.

value investing

An approach to picking stocks based on actual value of the company rather than on price or price targets.

vega

A name sometimes applied to the calculation of tau.

volatility

An indicator of the degree of change in a stock's market value, measured over a 12-month period and stated as a percentage. To measure volatility, subtract the lowest 12-month price from the highest 12-month price, and divide the answer by the 12-month lowest price.

volume

The level of trading activity in a stock, an option, or the market as a whole.

wash sale rule

A provision in the tax code prohibiting the deduction of a loss if the security position is reopened within 30 days from the date of the sale.

wasting asset

Any asset that declines in value over time. An option is an example of a wasting asset because it exists only until expiration, after which it becomes worthless.

writer

The individual who sells (writes) a call or a put.

RECOMMENDED READING

Cohen, Guy. *Options Made Easy*. Upper Saddle River, NJ: Financial Times/Prentice Hall, 2002.

Johnston, S. A. *Trading Options to Win: Profitable Strategies and Tactics for Any Trader*. Hoboken, NJ: John Wiley & Sons, 2003.

Kolb, Robert W. *Understanding Options*. New York: John Wiley & Sons, 2001.

McMillan, Lawrence G. *McMillan on Options,* 2nd ed. Hoboken, NJ: John Wiley & Sons, 2004.

Olmstead, W. Edward. *Options for the Beginner and Beyond: Unlock the Opportunities and Minimize the Risks*. Upper Saddle River, NJ: Financial Times/Practice Hall, 2006.

Schaeffer, Bernie. *The Option Advisor*. New York: John Wiley & Sons, 1997.

Sincere, Michael. *Understanding Options*. New York: McGraw–Hill, 2006.

Thomsett, Michael C. *Options Trading for the Conservative Investor*. Upper Saddle River, NJ: Financial Times/Prentice Hall, 2005.

Wolfinger, Mark D. *The Rookie's Guide to Options*. Cedar Falls, IA: W & A Publishing, 2008.

ABOUT THE AUTHOR

MICHAEL C. THOMSETT (www.MichaelThomsett.com) has written more than 70 books on investing, real estate, business, and management. He is author of several Wiley books, including the eight editions of the bestselling *Getting Started in Options*, as well as *Getting Started in Fundamental Analysis, Getting Started in Real Estate Investing*, and *Getting Started in Swing Trading*. He also has written numerous other stock investing and trading books, including *Winning with Stocks* (Amacom Books), *Stock Profits* (FT Press), and *Mastering Fundamental Analysis* and *Mastering Technical Analysis* (Dearborn Press). The author contributes regularly to many websites, including the CBOE, Benzinga, Seeking Alpha and on his website, ThomsettOptions.com; and writes articles for the *AAII Journal* and NAIC's *Better Investing*. He also teaches five classes at the New York Institute of Finance (NYIF). Thomsett has been writing professionally since 1978 and full time since 1985. He lives near Nashville, Tennessee.

INDEX